For my children.

MARY McKAY

....

How Our Mental Healthcare
System Fails Us

A Mother's Personal Reflections
and Cry for Help

....

Swimming
Lessons

Library of Congress Cataloging-in-Publication Data available.

ISBN: 978-0-692-75638-6
Printed in the United States of America

Book design:
Peter Gloege / LOOK Design Studio

Editorial development and creative design support by Ascent:
www.itsyourlifebethere.com

Follow Mary McKay:
 mary.mckay357   @marymckay3
www.truthaccordingtomary.blogspot.com

Acknowledgments

This book would not exist were it not for my friendship with Paula Alford, who has been with me on this journey every step of the way and understands more than anyone outside my family. She is the reason I met David Hazard, who also understands in his special way. Without his knowledgeable and supportive coaching and his sensitivity throughout this process I could not have finished this project. I would not be a writer at all, were it not for the steadfast support and encouragement of my husband and children. Above all, I love and admire them all for their strength during our most difficult days, and for their courage in sharing our story.

Contents

PREFACE

You gotta swim
Swim in the dark
There's no shame in drifting
Feel the tide shifting and wait for the spark
Yeah you've gotta swim
Don't let yourself sink
Just find the horizon
I promise you it's not as far as you think.

—"SWIM" BY JACK'S MANNEQUIN

As a kid I took swimming lessons and passed, but then in my mid-teens there was this near-drowning incident at a beach with unexpected surf and undertow. I panicked and began to go under. A stranger dragged me out, then disappeared.

When I decided to write this book, the image of fighting a tide came to my mind, and thus the title. To navigate the world when your child is mentally ill is to swim for your life.

It also helps to be positive.

Before you read my story, know that I tell it not to get sympathy. I want parents, family members, friends, teachers, neighbors, politicians, and treating professionals to know what it has been like "in the trenches" over the last two decades dealing with mental illness, so that we can all make demands for specific changes, while acknowledging improvements that are happening but that are too slow in coming. More importantly, I want parents to hold onto hope. There are good reasons for hope in 2016. The changes that are happening in the developments in technology in medicine and behavioral health bode well for the future, but there is no fast fix coming. Parents of mentally ill children need to know that no matter what sorrows and pain are coming their way, they can stay afloat and keep swimming even in the deepest water if they never let go of hope. I'm a bit like Nellie in *South Pacific*: a cockeyed optimist, "stuck like a dope with this thing called hope."

Hope is good medicine. And it's free.

I'm not sure what exists beyond this life, but I do know that heaven and hell both exist on earth. I have learned that hell is not the opposite of heaven; the great thing about hell is that it allows you to recognize heaven when you see it. I know because I have been to both places in my life, and know I will return to each as my journey continues. Life goes forward, and joy and pain are the tidal pools in which we, suddenly, may find ourselves.

Cockeyed or not, I'm not delusional. I am not a Pollyanna playing "the glad game." Here's what I know: With a mentally ill child, there will always be abyss moments, and I've had plenty. The short version of my story is that I am the mother of four grown children. Two of them developed mental illness at an early age, and that meant over twenty years of doctors, counselors, frustrated teachers, psych and educational testing, expert consultations with specialists far and near, and trips to the county courthouse. There were shocks, screams, tears, and more tears. Money flushed. Nights without sleep. Headlong crashes into stone walls of inescapable, deadly reality.

Still, my children have always been beautiful, and my love for them without limit. While this is my story, it is their story too, and they have encouraged me to tell it. Their desire to share about themselves in order to encourage understanding is amazing to me. Setbacks continue, but my hope for the future remains strong.

I keep swimming.

INTRODUCTION

*I*n the fall of 2013, a fifty-five-year-old father in Virginia was stabbed several times in the face and upper body by his twenty-four-year-old son. The young man then turned a gun on himself. The father survived; the son died. *The Washington Post* reported that the young man had become increasingly troubled, showing signs of "paranoia, deep suspicions about schemes to undermine or conspire against him, manic highs and deep lows." The day before the incident, his father had obtained an emergency custody order to have a mental health evaluation, but his son was released because a survey across a wide area of the state located no psychiatric bed for him. This story made the national news because the father is a prominent, respected Virginia politician and former candidate for governor: Creigh Deeds.

* * *

"The victims of mental illness are crying out to us—loudly, publicly, and covered in blood. This has got to be the year that we listen." Petula Dvorak, 1/20/2014 in *The Washington Post*: "Ignoring Mental Illness Won't Make it Go Away."

* * *

The National Alliance on Mental Illness (NAMI) quotes the Surgeon General's report "that 10 percent of children and adolescents in the United States suffer from serious emotional and mental disorders that cause significant functional impairment in their day-to-day lives at home, in school and with peers." The American Psychiatric Association reports that some 8000 child and adolescent psychiatrists care for about 20–30 million young people with serious mental illness.

* * *

The National Association of Community Health Centers reports that persons living with mental illness have a higher mortality rate and often die prematurely from preventable diseases such as diabetes, cardiovascular disease, respiratory diseases, and infectious diseases. They are more likely to engage in smoking, drug and alcohol abuse, and unsafe sexual behavior. They have a higher rate of poor nutrition, obesity, and lack of exercise. To address these problems, there are far too few community medical centers, and not all of them provide mental health counseling and treatment. Only 40 percent provide substance abuse treatment, and only 20 percent offer twenty-four-hour crisis intervention service.

* * *

I have lived in and raised my four children in Northern Virginia near the nation's capital for more than thirty years. As a parent and a teacher, I was involved in public, private, and parochial schools as well as in local, state, and national politics. I have an undergraduate degree in psychology and a master's in education. Despite a fortunate background, I have been navigating the mental health system for decades because of a need in my own family. The term "navigation" here is used loosely; it has been more like riding a canoe on whitewater rapids without a paddle.

For example, only when I began writing this book did I learn of the existence of a law here in Virginia called the Comprehensive Services Act, which years ago could have provided information and services to help our family. I've been told by an expert in the field, "Don't feel bad. No one knows about it."

* * *

In January of 2014, Jacquelyn Martin, an Associated Press photographer, was taking random pictures around Washington, D.C. One photo, of a scruffy, dazed young man bundled up on a freezing day warming himself near a heat grate, was published in *USA Today* and widely circulated. By pure random luck, his family saw the photo and located their missing son, who had recently gone missing from their home in upstate New York. Take note: Every "crazy" person on the street is not without people who care. "Martin said the episode serves as a reminder to journalists that every person they encounter has a story to tell." (*The Washington Post*)

CHAPTER ONE

How to Have a Perfect Family

*H*ere is where I plead guilty to having been an arrogant know-it-all/know-nothing at the beginning of my adult life. I believed I knew the secret to having a perfect family.

It began with the idea that I could do a better job than my parents did with my three siblings and me. While they did their best to raise us, my parents' "best" was limited by the heavy baggage they brought from their own childhoods: poverty, ignorance, divorce, abandonment, alcoholism, violence. Their main life goals were based on having left behind their ethnic lower-class beginnings in a New England factory town and rising to the heights of upper-middle-class living through my father's military career. Becoming parents was not a plan or choice; it was just life for a Catholic couple without birth control. As parents, they were strict and sometimes physically cruel and indifferent about some things that should have mattered more. As we grew older, they were quick to criticize and slow to hug.

When I went off to college at seventeen and majored in psychology, it was because I had some vague sense of "doing something to help people." Mostly I just wanted to understand behavior I was observing in my peers and why it seemed I was the "strong" one they came to for advice. For a career, I thought I might become a social worker. When I graduated, it was with only a bit of knowledge and little true understanding about what made everyone around me tick. More importantly, I was still clueless about the fact that my family of origin was a contributing factor to my own personal issues, as well as my interest in psychology and desire to help people.

As I moved into the adult world of career, marriage, and eventually parenthood, I was dismayed to gradually realize that all families were not like my family, and that mine had been dysfunctional in many ways. I came to believe that my parents were deeply flawed, and that their mistakes caused the dysfunctional environment in which my siblings and I grew up. I loved them despite their failures, but became determined that when I had my own children, I would be a different kind of parent. My children would turn out right.

I had so much to learn.

Over the course of my life I have come to understand that there is no perfect family. Most families have their own dysfunction. No matter how "normal" a family appears to an outsider, its dynamic is much like stones tossed into a lake: the smooth-as-glass surface cannot possibly remain so with all the overlapping and blending disturbances we benignly refer to as "ripples." For some families, those ripples are huge waves that never dissipate. When someone talks about their crazy family—the critical mother, the manipulative sibling, the hyperactive kid, the remote father, the disastrous and painfully hilarious family vacations and holidays—I now understand that "crazy" is on a long continuum that reaches from "quirky" to catastrophic, but only a few (if any) are lucky enough to avoid that continuum altogether.

In fact, if you exist, I want to meet you.

I thought my youthful interest in psychology and social work was purely academic. I never wanted to be a firsthand expert in mental illness, behavioral treatments, psychotropic medications, addiction, and family dysfunction. Alas, I am. For many years I have lived in an alternate universe far from the positive, uplifting "helping people" dream of my youth and my naïve plans for perfect parenthood.

Keeping Secrets

It's humiliating to admit your household isn't perfect, as you imagine everyone else's is.

In the decades before the Internet and Facebook, I kept family and friends apprised of the wondrous things happening behind my front door through an annual Christmas letter. Yes, as a writer I was compelled to send out the kind of nauseating rundown of all our accomplishments for the year, punctuated with lots of exclamation points. But then life got harder, and it was a challenge to share with others. The first year I skipped sending out Christmas greetings it was because I was a cancer patient, enduring surgery, chemotherapy, and radiation. I didn't want pity. As my children grew to become teenagers, I skipped a few more years because it was becoming harder on my creative nonfiction to work around alcohol overdoses, fits of temper, car wrecks, poor grades, changing schools, suicide threats, sneaking out, smoking cigarettes, school skipping, and more. No one else should know about the hefty amount of time and money being spent on psychotherapists and medications. In fact, for many years it felt as though our family kept the entire mental health industry afloat, but that wasn't something I wanted to broadcast during the happiest season of the year.

Only a few people knew most of my family secrets. Over time, as my situation became increasingly disturbing, with no letup and no solutions, I became reluctant to share my unending tale of woe with anyone. I began to fear it might alienate even those I was closest to. Others had to be tired of hearing my troubles. Even I was tired of myself and my problems. Gradually, I turned inward.

Keeping secrets doesn't help us. A counseling mantra is "we are only as sick as our secrets." I do know that talking about our stories is better than hiding and furthering the stigma. Perhaps the popularity and value of reality shows like *Honey*

Boo Boo, *Real Housewives*, and *Keeping Up with the Kardashians* is to reassure the rest of us that all manner of weird stuff goes on behind the front door of every home. There is no "normal."

I am a survivor. Now I know that the right thing to do is to tell my story and encourage others to tell theirs. Silence helps no one. To be blunt, the stigma of "crazy" is a boil that must be lanced, and I want to do my part to sharpen the scalpel. Telling my story may show others how bad things can get in this journey, yet also demonstrate that parents can navigate even the most horrific circumstances. I share the mistakes I made in looking for help in a system that is broken, and offer recommendations for how the system could work better. In the meantime, I hope that such information may save other parents from wasting time, money, and emotion on dead ends. Parents must recognize that others make mistakes as well; here I hold up a mirror to all treating professionals, teachers, special education administrators, and others who would judge and criticize a struggling kid or his parents. My story may liberate other families to see that they are not alone in facing the daunting task of raising a child with mental illness, and to know that it is possible to find good help. Ultimately, I want to help families not lose sight of all that is good and lovable in life as well as in their difficult child.

CHAPTER TWO

Blame or Credit the Parents

*"If you bungle raising your children,
I don't think whatever else you do well
matters very much."*

—JACQUELINE KENNEDY ONASSIS

No one needs to tell a parent that success in life is complete only if you can also claim credit for raising excellent children as well. Jacqueline Kennedy was admired around the world. As a parent, she did her best in highly unusual circumstances, and if a tenth of the tabloid gossip was true, her children were not perfect. From the beginning of Bill Clinton's campaign to win the presidency, even those who accused him and Hillary of the most heinous personal and political conduct were forced to grudgingly acknowledge and give them credit for the fact that their daughter Chelsea turned out so well.

Blame Sigmund Freud and Dr. Benjamin Spock for starting this interconnectedness—the whole thing about parents being credited or blamed for how their children turn out. Though it is somewhat taboo to actually say it out loud, there is tsk-tsking going on among observers if someone's child breaks bad. Why not? Isn't it just like blaming the chef if you don't like the soup? Isn't raising a child a simple matter of following the right recipe? You mix ingredients, bake at 350 degrees, and *voila*. But be careful! A little too much garlic or baking time, and you will produce a disaster.

It's a thrill for parents to pat themselves on the back if their kids do well. For Baby Boomer parents, the accomplishments of the children are a direct reflection of the narcissism and navel-gazing characteristic of that (okay, okay, *my*) generation. But in recent years, there have been rising numbers of learning disabled, mentally ill, or other "special needs" children. While the causes of this trend are not definitively understood (and it is possible it is simply that we are more aware of such difficulties) parents of disturbed children are now told: "It's not your fault." "You didn't cause this." "Don't beat yourself up." "You did your best." Soothing comments of professionals and support groups to ease the suffering and give parents permission to put down the burden of blame. It seldom works. Just as you proudly say "That's my boy!" when he hits a home run in Little League, you find yourself humbly apologizing, "Oh, I'm SO SORRY!" when your kid gets in trouble for biting in preschool or has been caught shoplifting at the mall. We may have permission to escape blame, but too often we still feel it's all about us.

The belief that parents have complete control over the outcomes of their children's lives is a dream, the receiving blanket of promise that wraps every newborn. The new parent looks at their baby and believes the future can't be anything but bright. However, that beautiful new creature who journeys to your arms arrives with luggage. His temperament and genetic predispositions may be fit for a different path than his parents have in mind. This isn't necessarily a bad thing. Your baby may grow to become a musical prodigy, a math geek, a computer whiz, a basketball star. One of my four kids proved at a young age to be highly gifted in mathematics. This was a surprise to his parents, since we both struggled to get through math in school. We are proud of our math genius, but can't take credit because we have no idea how he got this natural ability. Apparently, some distant relative's DNA contains a gene for mathematics, or (as is a running family joke) maybe the hospital sent the wrong baby home with us.

So, DNA = Destiny?

Is DNA the final determinant of destiny? Is the pendulum swinging to the other extreme now, absolving parents of all responsibility? No. The answer is somewhere in between.

Recent research may reinforce the idea that nurture may be as important as nature after all. In her 2014 *New York Times* article "Redefining Mental Illness," T.M. Luhrman discusses current research that is looking at the biology of neurological structures first, and secondly at psychiatric symptoms, which is a reversal of labeling a person with a diagnosis and then trying to treat it with medications. For example, a person with anxiety might have her "fear circuitry" studied first. In addition, Luhrman believes in some theories emerging now back to the idea that social factors play a role in symptoms and away from seeing them as a DNA/biology related disease of the brain. In a letter to the editor in response to Luhrman's article, psychiatrist Dr. Michael Lustick, medical director of the Parent Child Resource Center in Connecticut and an assistant clinical professor at Yale who has twenty-five years of experience in treating children and adolescents, strongly supports this this new approach. He eloquently states that, *"psychiatric conditions and life narratives inform each other"* (emphasis added).

Another expert in the field of mental illness and a depression sufferer herself, Therese Borchard, writes that, "… the new science of epigenetics, the study of external changes made to the DNA that turn our genes 'on' or 'off,' can help moms feel better. When I find myself saying, *Did you really think you could have children who didn't inherit your junk? How cruel of you to bring kids into this world, knowing full well that they may suffer the way you do*, I remember that volumes of research suggest that just because someone is born with genes that predispose him to a lot of suffering does not mean the little kid will suffer. What scientists have discovered in the last ten years is that we can actually control how our genes express themselves."

The bottom line here is fuzzy. This is not an exact science. As far as is understood at this point, it seems genetics are like Forrest Gump's box of chocolates: You never know what you're going to get. As a parent, you can enjoy the whole box or only savor the ones you like best and hope there aren't too many with a surprise filling not to your liking.

Okay, so let's assume that parenting does matter.

You're the Parent, But You Are Not Totally in Charge

I tried to do everything right. We waited until we were married five years before we decided we were ready to be parents. We had established our careers and bought, decorated, and furnished a new condo, and we weren't yet thirty. The kids were planned and cherished from dream to conception to birth and onward. I was blessed with easy pregnancies, easy births, and babies who slept through the night at a few weeks of age. It was so easy!

So I did it four times.

Over the course of twenty years, I was mostly a stay-at-home mom. I should have had my mail delivered to the minivan. I drove carpools and chauffeured noisy gangs of boys and girls to playgrounds and play dates, sports practices and games, dance lessons and birthday parties. I took up residence in classrooms and sports fields, made costumes and cupcakes, edited school newsletters, served on the boards of parent-teacher organizations, and ran fundraisers. In my adult world, such as it was, I was fortunate that my husband's career afforded me the freedom to go in and out of the paid workforce through occasional free-lance, temporary, and part-time positions. I took classes. Taught

Sunday school. Volunteered in political campaigns. Earned a master's degree. I helped my husband with the social end of his corporate career and traveled with him often. I plead guilty to being addicted to busy. As our family grew, sometimes I felt overwhelmed and underappreciated, but I was never bored.

My husband and I made conscious decisions about what our children were exposed to when they were young. In retrospect, we probably went overboard. No television or movies containing sex, violence, drug references, or bad language. There were no real or toy guns in our home, and no gunplay. (We did, of course, allow pretend laser battles of *Star Wars*-obsessed little boys.) In the summer, we spent two weeks hanging out on a rocky beach on a small New England island, fishing, swimming, sunning, and collecting shells and beach glass. When they weren't in school, I regularly took my kids to the National Zoo and the Smithsonian museums. Almost every Christmas we traveled to Disney World. There was no drinking or smoking in our house. We took them to church and made sure they got a religious education. We encouraged extracurricular activities to keep them busy with healthy pursuits: they tried soccer, swimming, baseball, football, tennis, and basketball. For a while there were music lessons that didn't last—one tried violin and saxophone, another tried drums, all tried piano. My daughter also took singing lessons, cheerleading, Irish dance, and ballet.

During their school years there were rules—so many rules. About schoolwork, curfews, and limitations on TV and video games. In high school, we required that they had to reach a B+ or better average in school to get a driver's license (which delayed three of them driving for several years, thank you). Senior year there was not even a discussion of Beach Week, the bacchanalia festival at the shore. They knew that was not going to happen. Of course, all our rules made us the weirdest, meanest parents ever. My daughter once accused us of wanting her to be Amish because of our rules about what she could wear: no pierced ears before age thirteen; no bikinis, spaghetti straps, tight jeans, tube tops, short skirts, or short shorts.

As opportunities came along to have "the sex talk," we gave honest answers to their questions. We encouraged them to pay close attention in family life ed in their schools (admittedly because we were grateful that most of their information would be handled by someone else, and couldn't imagine why anyone would take the "opt-out" choice). We thought the movie *Mean Girls* nailed it: The gym teacher's total sex-ed lesson was, "Don't have sex. You'll get pregnant. You'll get AIDS. And you'll die." We told our kids to have respect for others and to appreciate the connections between love, marriage, and parenthood. Oh, and condoms.

My husband and I weren't totally consumed with our kids. Babysitters were expensive and sometimes hard to find, but kept us sane. Often, we took time to go out (just us) to movies, or spend a weekend away. We considered it healthy for us to be alone and for them to spend a few hours with a babysitter, or a few days with their grandmother.

Our house was noisy, messy, and chaotic at times. All those rules? Constantly broken, of course. The kids spent plenty of angry moments in time-out on the stairs, and later with lost privileges. When we were up to six members, sometimes we were like a herd of over-caffeinated goats. My memory is of a joyful kind of exhaustion from all the activity and laughter when my kids were young. When I look at the old home movies we made with the Buick-sized video camera my husband toted everywhere, I see lots of fun and warmth, humor, and love. Every day was an adventure.

It's been said, "The bigger the kid, the bigger the problem," and it proved true in our household. As time went by and the kids grew older, the fun and the laughter were sometimes outweighed by anger, frustration, and even horror. In hindsight, we recognize that we were not perfect; we made some mistakes. Too much yelling. Too much sarcasm and too many put-downs. But I have now come to understand and accept that with all I tried to do to influence my children's upbringing, I wasn't totally in charge anyway. No one can say what influences affected the mysterious DNA in each of our children. Eventually, in spite of, or because of, our parenting, they became themselves.

Parenting is a job that requires no permission, no training, no license, no background checks. There is no minimum or maximum age limit, education, or income level. And this isn't China—you can have as many kids as you like. Parenting is the ultimate in on-the-job-training. We all know people who should not be parents, but there are many cases where bad parenting does not lead to a bad outcome. And, unfortunately, even good parenting sometimes ends in tragedy. It is important to accept that good parenting is good enough, even if the kid doesn't turn out to be what you hoped. All you can do is your best, while keeping mindful that so little is actually within your control. My own parents made mistakes, but it is impossible to say which mistakes may have led to which problem in any of their children. My parents did their best with the raw material they had. Ultimately, we became ourselves, in spite of, or because of, anything they did. I do know that of their four children, only one suffered serious brain illness. My brother had learning disabilities, emotional problems, and drug addiction. He died at age fifty from health problems linked to these fundamental problems he had all his life. But what roles did genetics and parenting play? That's impossible to determine.

As a mother I was thoughtful, empathetic, and educated about the minutiae of children's needs. I was "meta-mom," self-aware at all times of the huge responsibility of parenting. Things did not turn out perfectly, even though I did my best. Now I have to accept that it was good enough.

CHAPTER THREE

Love and Parenting

"Soon madness has worn you down. It's easier to do what it says than argue. In this way, it takes over your mind. You no longer know where it ends and you begin. You believe anything it says. You do what it tells you, no matter how extreme or absurd. If it says you're worthless, you agree. You plead for it to stop. You promise to behave. You are on your knees before it, and it laughs."

—MARYA HORNBACHER, *Madness: A Bipolar Life*

My daughter has an illness. Because she is sick with something that manifests itself in inappropriate behavioral symptoms rather than a rash or fever, people don't understand. They treat her badly. In the grip of an illness that can't be cured or wished away, she tries to live as normally as she can, while her perceptions and emotions cycle and lurch and crash like bumper cars at an amusement park.

* * *

Love is the path to satisfy the yearning of our spirit to be connected. There are scientific theories among those who immerse themselves in quantum mechanics that love exists among all humankind because consciousness exists separate from our corporal existence. Viewed this way, we can believe we are connected, inseparable, and so we can change or fix another person. Especially our child, who we thought was a *tabula rasa* at birth, a blank slate, and with the right amount of love he would grow to be a perfect human being.

In the 2010 novel *Room,* a mother and her five-year-old son are prisoners in a locked shed for years and are bonded in a way that is functional in dysfunctional circumstances. Emma Donaghue, the author, says "Really, everything in *Room* is just a defamiliarisation of ordinary parenthood . . . The idea was to focus on the primal drama of parenthood the way from moment to moment you swing from comforter to tormentor, just as kids simultaneously light up our lives and drive us nuts. I was trying to capture that strange, bipolar quality of parenthood. For all that being a parent is normal statistically, it's not normal psychologically. It produces some of the most extreme emotions you'll ever have" (*The Guardian*, 2010).

Anyone who has loved another must accept the nearly impossible: Even with tight emotional bonds, the "other" is separate and unique, not an extension of you. Nothing but pain results if you try too hard to make that loved one into someone else. Unfortunately, most of us compulsively do that anyway, especially when it comes to our children. We need to believe that we can control our child forever as easily as when he was a baby kept safe in a car when we buckled him into his car seat.

Too often, parents devote their lives to a fruitless search to "fix" their child, as I did, for years. At times it has consumed my life. Changing doctors, changing schools, changing treatments, changing medications; all have been as curative as changing clothes. I was swimming against the tide and getting nowhere, yet I could not stop. I loved my little girl so. How could I not do everything to help her become closer to "normal"?

The Four C's

The hardest ideas to accept when you have an "imperfect" child can be referred to as "the 4 Cs."

- » You didn't cause it.
- » You can't control it.
- » You can't cure it.
- » You can, however, contribute to the problems.

I came late to this concept, and I still can't always accept it. I still sometimes wonder, did I cause my daughter's problems? Is this punishment for my desire for a girl, instead of being satisfied with my three little boys? Was she so cherished that I spoiled her? Did the bump on her head I didn't prevent when she was nine months old and fell on the brick fireplace lead to brain damage? Were all the psychiatric medications a mistake? Did they make things worse? Was I wrong to encourage her to ride a bike when I knew she had coordination deficiencies and might take a fall or two? Was her broken femur my fault for trying to make her "normal"? So many questions can only be managed by thinking about the four Cs.

* * *

I was in Labor Room #7, my lucky number, when they placed her in my arms, all perfect nine pounds of her. I adored my three boys, who were then nine, six, and three, but by then I wanted a girl so badly I wouldn't let the doctors tell me the sex from sonograms because I didn't want to feel disappointed. I tried not to think about pink.

But then, miraculously it seemed, here she was. A daughter! I can't even put into words the joy.

As I looked into the perfect, rosy little newborn, oh the dreams I had! In my fantasy world, a world I was only barely conscious of, she would be a new and improved version of . . . me. This new baby girl would be smarter and prettier. She'd wear better clothes, have more toys, go to better schools. She was adored, and she would know it, always. With three older brothers, she would always be protected. And there would be no shortage of nice boys to meet when she was old enough. Everything would be wonderful.

Katherine was a vocal baby from her first days, with an almost constant run of baby gibberish. Real words began around her first birthday, and she hasn't stopped to take a breath yet. As a toddler we'd laugh. It was cute. Her vocabulary was impressive, charming. Then.

As she got older, it became troublesome. Every thought that went through her mind came out of her mouth. It became embarrassing in public. Once, when she was three, I had a part-time job in a high-level government office and had to take her to work with me because the babysitter cancelled at the last minute. I had no choice but to take her into the morning staff meeting, knowing disaster was ahead, but hoping for the best. She took over and wouldn't stop talking. My coworkers, all childless, politely smiled. I wanted to disappear. Another time, caught in a wall-to-wall crowd at Disney World, she was begging for something and I said, "No." She shouted, "SO! You wish I was dead! JESUS TAKE ME NOW!" Heads turned and stared. Redfaced, I gamely tried to explain, "She's just kidding!" Once, when she was six, the entire family was cooped up in the car on a long drive with her nonstop chatter. Trying to get her to stop made her mad and it got worse. Now we all were angry, and punishment was promised. Finally, exasperated, I offered her an out. "Katherine, if you want to get out of trouble, the FIRST thing you have to do is STOP TALKING!" After a pause, she said, "What's the SECOND thing?"

She was born for the stage. She began singing when she was a toddler in a car seat, singing with Gloria Estefan and Shania Twain on the radio. At two, she could recite an entire book called *Are You My Mother?* with various inflections and voices. In preschool and kindergarten productions, she would take over the front row, singing her heart out with performance art in her expressions and movements, while her little classmates wandered or stood in confusion. As a pre-teen, she began her own karaoke party every day in the bathroom mirror, singing to her CDs. She became a beautiful and talented young lady, and she was happy.

But school was becoming increasingly difficult. It began in first grade when she had trouble learning to read. She was referred to the county education system for testing. That is when we received the shocking news that she had severe learning disabilities, especially in math and visual-spatial skills. We did not believe it. Something had to be wrong with the test. We had her retested (at great expense) by an outside expert. Results were the same. Here is where we first heard terms about "special education" and "schools for kids with disabilities."

We were devastated. She was so charismatic and outgoing and verbal! How could this be true? We were experienced parents with three other children and hadn't seen this coming.

Of course, we recognized that she was accident prone. Her klutziness was part of the profile, not part of normal development. She tended to falls; she broke her right arm at age two, her left arm at age three. At eleven, she had a serious bicycle accident in which she suffered a head injury and a broken femur. What followed was a year of recovery: a wheelchair, then crutches, surgeries, and physical therapy. Things began to change. She lost confidence, developed anxiety and depression, had serious problems with peers, and began to avoid going to school.

She still loved drama and singing, but only in private. To my surprise, when she was fourteen she asked if she could attend a local acting audition. I agreed, despite my doubts about her ability to carry herself on stage. Hundreds of kids and parents crowded the hotel where they held the event. Katherine didn't seem nervous at all (I was a wreck, fearing she would humiliate herself). At one point a judge asked, "Do any of you sing?" and she raised her hand. They asked her to sing to the crowd of parents and kids outside in the hallway. Unprepared, untrained, unpracticed, she launched into a stunning *a capella* version of "Ready to Run" by the Dixie Chicks. When she finished, the crowd stood and burst into enthusiastic applause. I beamed through tears and said, "That's my daughter!"

* * *

It is clear to me now that a child arrives not a blank slate, but a slate with some artwork and a few words and numbers already on it, and some of those letters and numbers may be upside down, or backwards. Our children are individuals, not extensions of ourselves. They are not always easy to love and accept, but when we become parents we are making a commitment to try. I wish I had known sooner that the best way to live is to savor each day, each bit of happiness, each proud "Ready to Run" moment. Now I remind myself every day not to devote a moment to regrets about the past or fear about the future, because doing so only robs me of the joy that may come today.

CHAPTER FOUR

Appearances are Deceiving

The signs were missed. The successful and wealthy parents thought all was normal with their youngest son, John, the quietest of their three children. When he began to withdraw as a high school student, staying in his room listening to Beatles records, they interpreted it as shyness. As time went on and he was unable to stay with a job or in college, they thought he was depressed. His parents consulted a psychiatrist and got the impression that their son was only immature, and in need of some tough love. They let him leave home and cut him off financially. Later, his father said, "I didn't think about mental illness, and I sent a helpless human being out into the world to try to cope when he was totally unable to cope."

That human being was John Hinckley, who shot President Reagan.

* * *

Senator George McGovern and his wife, Eleanor, did all they could to save their daughter Terry. She died at age forty-five after a lifelong struggle with depression and alcoholism. She was found frozen to death in a snowbank, after having recently left her sixty-eighth stint at inpatient treatment. In the last six months of her life, they took the advice of a counselor and distanced themselves from her. As he wrote in his book, *Terry: My Daughter's Life and Death Struggle with Alcoholism*, "Tough love turns the lives around of many, but when it does not work it has the potential to doom the survivors to decades of self-doubt and agony." For the rest of his life, the senator suffered from guilt about having abandoned his daughter and contributing to her death. In his book about Terry, he said he regretted his action: "There is no such thing as too much compassion, understanding, support and love for the sick and dying."

* * *

We were traveling out of the country when we received an urgent phone call in the middle of the night. Our son, Brendan, then a college freshman, was in a hospital ICU in a coma from an overdose of some unidentifiable drug. He had returned to his dorm from a party Friday night and gone to bed, and he seemed to be sleeping all the next day. By Saturday night, his roommate found him on the floor. He and another student tried and failed to wake him up, so they called 911, and he was taken away by ambulance.

The doctor advised us to arrive quickly; he had already restarted Brendan's heart twice and couldn't guarantee whether he would survive. In numbing terror, we got on the next plane to Dulles Airport, dropped off our other children with friends, and then drove two hours to Richmond to the hospital. When we arrived, he was still critical, but, miraculously, he was now improving. I will never forget how fragile my six-foot-six boy looked in the ICU. After he recovered, he couldn't remember anything beyond attending the party. The doctors told him he had almost died, and Brendan joked, "I'll have to be more careful in the future!"

He was young. It would be years before he got scared straight.

* * *

Through the Front Door, a Drop into an Abyss

I have been fortunate. If you were to visit my home, you would see a lovely, upper middle-class, split-level house with a long driveway and lots of tall trees in a wealthy suburb of Washington, D.C. It is safe area, and one of the strongest school districts in the country. Inside my house you would see antiques, oil paintings, New England memorabilia, oriental rugs, and souvenirs from favorite places we have travelled, such as London, Paris, and Italy; a Brunello wine collection, flat screen HD televisions in several rooms, and a garage and basement overstuffed with boxes of things compiled over thirty-nine years of marriage and the raising of four children. We are among the affluent.

On the heirloom baby grand piano (which no one plays and long ago went out of tune) and various other shelves and walls you would see lots of family pictures stretching from the 1940s to the present, documenting the history of our family in smiles: my parents on the day they eloped in 1953; my husband and his cousin, both skinny and buzz-cut boys hanging out on the front porch in the summer of 1962; all four of our beautiful children on the Christmas card we sent in 1991; my parents in their dotage, holding hands on a beach; my husband and I at Bill Clinton's inauguration in 1992; my in-laws on their wedding day in 1950; my youngest son at age eight, meeting Pope John-Paul II; the wedding of my oldest son in 2012. Graduations, baptisms, reunions, holidays, anniversaries, and other occasions that document the happiness of family life. One of my favorites is the eight-by-ten of my daughter at fifteen, stunningly beautiful as she was heading out to a high school homecoming dance. Her eyes are bright, her smile wide, her pale, flawless skin and blonde hair the perfect accompaniments to a white and gold strapless dress. I remember that night so clearly. How she sparkled!

Then, over several years, there was a slide into an abyss that we failed to halt no matter what we did, and I think we did everything possible. That fresh-faced, smiling fifteen-year-old became in a few years time a tattooed, pierced, skeletal, physically ill, ratty haired, physically and emotionally scarred homeless person, nearly unrecognizable as a member of our family. At the same time, her brother Brendan, who had suffered from anxiety since elementary school, sank into the world of addiction, spending time in an out of rehabs.

There are no photos on the piano about any of this.

The insanity of this situation became a routine part of our life within the walls of our home. It would horrify the few friends in whom we would confide the truth. Under our roof, four people were living happy, predictable, successful lives, succeeding in school and careers, going to proms and graduations and college, winning awards, traveling to Europe and Florida and the Caribbean, eating out, buying cars and clothes, playing with our beloved dogs—a "normal" American life. And two other members of our family were choosing to live in poverty, sometimes on the street, disappearing for weeks and months at a time, surviving somehow with no home, no food, no family, no money. Adrift in the world of the homeless shelter, the crack house, a stranger's couch or floor or car; spending time in and out of an alien world of criminals, hallucinating psychotics, and desperate addicts.

For me, there were too many nights without rest; broken sleep wrapped in nightmares. The word "fear" doesn't cover it when you are wondering where your child is, and knowing it can't be a good place. I lived in constant terror of THE PHONE CALL: "Your child is dead."

Brendan was tall and street smart, with survivor skills, but Katherine was learning disabled and frail. She carried no wallet or ID of any kind, and I feared her future was to be an unsolved case of a Jane Doe in the morgue and that awful phone call would never reach us.

Even though we didn't know where Brendan or Katherine might be at any point, for the rest of us life went on in seemingly regular fashion. Often, we laughed.

I guess we were excellent at compartmentalization.

When people who knew our situation would ask, "How do you do it?" I'd shrug. And think of Everest. Why do they climb it? We have to. Because it's there.

CHAPTER FIVE

The Abyss

"Learning is a gift; even when pain is your teacher."

—MAYA WATSON

*I*t is difficult to explain how parents can live day to day when their child is mentally ill. When you open your eyes each morning you don't know what you are facing. Your child may be a pleasant and cooperative angel, or you could be dealing with a monster. It could be described as a roller coaster ride, except that at least on a roller coaster you can see the drops and turns coming and have a moment to prepare. Not so with mental illness.

For me, every time there was a period of peace and normalcy, I expected it to last. When something bad would happen, I would say, to myself, "It can't get worse."

My learning curve was flat as a pancake.

Keening

Sometimes a primal scream comes out of nowhere, harkening back to infancy when a wail was the only way to communicate pain, hunger, or a need. It came over me only once during this journey with my daughter. It was the moment when the severity of what we were facing hit me over the head.

It is important to note here that, incredibly, my primal scream happened before many, much worse things happened. I fell to pieces on an occasion that was *before* she:

> » Ran away a dozen times.
>
> » Confessed to drinking, drugging, and promiscuous sex.
>
> » Needed a Depo Provera birth control shot every four months.
>
> » Tried to quit high school repeatedly and had to be tutored to a diploma at age twenty.
>
> » Enrolled in community college, quit after two days, and disappeared for a week.
>
> » Got hired at several jobs and then quit or got fired within days.
>
> » Made several false claims of pregnancy.
>
> » Was raped.
>
> » Began to talk regularly about suicide, and made several halfhearted attempts.
>
> » Lived in a car for six weeks with a boyfriend.
>
> » Lived in various homeless shelters far from home.
>
> » Was beaten and nearly killed by a boyfriend.
>
> » Was held hostage at gunpoint by yet another.
>
> » Stopped taking birth control and got pregnant

» Eloped with a boyfriend, and later left her husband and baby and disappeared with a guy who was just out of jail.

» Got pregnant with another baby by him, a guy who fed her drugs when she was pregnant and is now serving time for drug dealing.

» Began cutting herself.

» Endured three hospitalizations in psych wards and many ER visits for various illnesses, including dehydration and starvation from being on the street.

» Contracted various STDs, including HIV.

» Was hospitalized (while pregnant) for two weeks and almost died of a severe infection requiring multiple tests, treatments, and two blood transfusions.

My primal scream came before all this and more happened to my beloved child. Let me repeat: Before all these horrors occurred, there was a moment when I thought my world had collapsed. In hindsight, I should have saved my scream for later.

* * *

From ages sixteen through eighteen, Katherine spent twenty months in a therapeutic wilderness boarding school, where she earned accolades, admiration, and love from the counselors, teachers, and other girls in the program. She was proud of herself when she left there, for never in her memory had she enjoyed such affirmation for anything. We all had such high hopes that she was finally on track to succeed, to finish high school and possibly even go on to college.

After her return, we learned quickly (and too late) that enrolling her in an ED (emotional disabilities) program at a large public high school among students who had drug and behavior problems was a mistake. Only a few weeks into the school year she confided to me that she had lost her virginity. It was her first boyfriend. He dropped her the next day, called her stupid, and spread the word all over class.

This tore my heart in pieces. How could this happen to my baby?

Primal scream then? NO. I tried to be cool. I was loving and understanding toward her, rationalizing to myself that she wasn't the first high school girl to sleep with the wrong boy. We talked about leaving this mistake behind, returning to a celibate life until someday when someone nice would come into her life who would truly love her. She seemed to agree. She began to wear her "true love waits" neck chain again.

But then, a few weeks later, she confided to me that she and another girl invited two boys into our basement for a sex party one Saturday night, while I was sleeping upstairs. I don't know why she told me, but oh, how I wished she hadn't!

That was the moment when I collapsed to the floor and began to scream. What remained of my optimism (actually: denial) about her becoming "cured" was gone. I saw how bad things were and now had a sense of how bad they would become. In Ireland they call it "keening," and it happens only at funerals. I keened for fifteen minutes, rocking back and forth as if on a drug-induced bad trip. If someone had just told me she was dead I would not have screamed louder or longer.

It felt like a death, because that was when I saw what was left of my vision for my daughter disappear in an avalanche of clarity. She was too emotionally ill and learning disabled to control her neediness for attention and a smile. She would become promiscuous; predatory males would use her like toilet paper and she wouldn't say no, or if she did say no, they would easily persuade her to do anything they wanted. Drinking, smoking, drugs, sex. She would do these things and she wouldn't understand why or how to say no. She would be a repeat victim of rape, and she wouldn't recognize it for what it was.

I would not be able to save her. I screamed until I couldn't scream any more.

Since that day, tears are constant, but invisible most of the time. They are there forever.

It was a school year from hell for us, where she began to skip school and disappear for days at a time. She took up cigarettes and drinking; she moved in with other families, telling them she was abused at home. Then she could engage in any behaviors she wanted without supervision. I would drive around our town looking for her, knocking on doors and calling the parents of other students. She would return from time to time and within days would be gone again. One night, a girlfriend of hers called to tell me Katherine was hanging out with some very bad people and in danger. I called the police. They tracked her down and brought her home. A female police officer sat her down for a kindly talk about her dangerous behaviors. Katherine was compliant, sweet, and polite. I thought her encounter with the police would frighten her into changing her risky behaviors. I was so grateful she was safe.

Within days she was gone again, and the pattern repeated—for the next five years.

But Still No Giving Up

In our family, we like to quote (and live by) a *Star Trek* reference: Captain Kirk, as a young Starfleet Academy cadet, is tested by the infamous "Kobayashi Maru Scenario," a final exam in which a starship captain must navigate a crisis that ultimately and intentionally has no winning solution. Kirk becomes the sole cadet to beat the program, explaining, "I don't believe in the 'no-win' scenario." That's us.

With Katherine, I knew what we were facing, but how could I allow her disabilities to defeat her? Growing up in this family, with our advantages, she had to be among those who would survive this, and survive it well. When her high school counselor advised us to begin the application process for her to receive Social Security Income, I ignored the suggestion. It seemed to me that this was an arbitrary and premature determination that Katherine would never hold a job. I kept believing her behaviors were a stage that she would outgrow.

(Side note: A few years later, when we finally did apply for SSI benefits, it took almost two years and one denial and appeal. At that point she certainly qualified, yet how could they deny her: learning disabled, homeless, mentally ill, HIV-positive, pregnant? I've only recently learned that apparently she could have been collecting SSI benefits from much earlier in her life, from the time she was deemed disabled. We had no idea—another example of how even a well-informed person immersed in this alternative universe can still have a massive lack of information.)

Things continued to worsen. It seemed she was on a path that could not be stopped. I prayed constantly: "Please don't let her get pregnant, God in heaven, please don't let her get pregnant!" Her counselors tried new approaches; her psychiatrists tried new medications and combinations of medications. The only ones she took for a length of time, lithium and Risperdal, did little to stop her behaviors, but made her gain weight and gave her tremors. Other meds seemed to do nothing.

I spent many hours at the library, on the Internet, and talking with other parents of children with special needs, searching for new ideas, new solutions. I was determined. There had to be some school or doctor or program or psychiatric medication that would make a difference. We tried everything we could find and afford financially that offered even the most remote chance of help. But everything I tried to micro-manage her life was as fruitless as a stage 4 cancer patient who "puts up a courageous fight, determined to beat the thing," and dies anyway.

Sometimes Parents Get Sick, Too

Something that I suffered in my twenties returned: panic attacks. My own emotional illness became unmanageable. I ignored the problems until I came to realize and admit that I needed help. I saw a psychiatrist, got on medication, and did two years in counseling.

For me, it wasn't just the stress and heartbreak. I was alternatively obsessed with solving the Katherine problem, and with every setback fantasizing about escaping my life. I didn't want to be her mother anymore. How do I resign this job? When that mother in Tennessee put her adopted son on a plane back to Russia, I totally understood her desperation. I dreamed about running away from home myself. Just disappear. I was emotionally sick, yes, but never suicidal or homicidal. I just wanted it all to stop.

My therapist asked me why I didn't just stop my over-involvement in my adult child's life, which was causing me a daily nightmare of mismanagement and failure as I lurched from this tactic to that one. My mission to outsmart and manipulate my kid until the problems went away was a battle that couldn't be won.

"Why are you doing this?" he asked me.

"Isn't it obvious? I'm trying to save her."

"Is it your job to do that? She's an adult."

"Doesn't a mother take on that job from the moment her baby is placed in her arms?"

"And when does it end?"

"I don't know."

"Do you really believe you can keep her, or her brother, alive?"

Silence. I hated when he was right.

In the end I had to think about this: Nothing I did for my daughter served *my* purposes, *my* needs. It's hard to face the fact that I have no power over mental illness, that it is a battle that cannot be won. Even now, with all I have learned and experienced, I struggle to accept and let go. Like any parent of any child, I take on each situation as best I can. With a child who has special needs like this, I have to bear in mind that there are good times in between the hits. I try, only sometimes successfully, to remember what a wise friend told me: Don't miss the wonder and enjoyment of the child you have, while wishing for a child that doesn't exist.

Love the Child; Hate the Illness

I will not get the perfect daughter of my dreams, but I do truly love the daughter I have. I hate her illness. I hate what it has done to her. But my love for her is deep and endless, because in her lucid moments, when she isn't angry, blaming her parents and everyone else, or fighting my efforts, her comments are heartbreaking:

"Mom, you have to play my music! If you can't like my music, it feels like you can't love me."

"I meet people and they like me. Then they get to know me and they tell me I'm crazy. They eventually disappear."

"Why do I have sex? Because I just want them to like me, even for just a few minutes."

"You all hate me because I'm such a mess. You all wish I would just go away."

"I might as well just kill myself."

The first twenty times she made suicidal threats, I tried to dismiss it as drama. Over time, she made a few half-hearted, unserious attempts that did no damage and were clearly a cry for attention and help. Then there were more serious attempts, such as trying to jump off an apartment balcony, an intentional overdose of drugs, and trying to hang herself with a belt. There were short-term hospitalizations. More recently, she has dealt with anxiety by cutting herself.

I know my daughter. She doesn't really want to die. But the responsibility to provide hope seems to fall on me. What if I fail? At times when I was most desperate and sick myself, the nauseating thought would creep into my mind like a fetid black ooze that if she kept talking of dying, maybe the poor wretch might be better off. More than once it has occurred to me that I certainly wouldn't want to live if I were in her shoes. Yet with all her suffering, she maintains a strong will to live.

* * *

When she was twenty years old, we were referred to an expert in the diagnosis and treatment of borderline personality disorder, Dr. Robert Freidel of the Virginia Commonwealth University medical center in Richmond. He had extensive personal experience with BPD and has authored several books on the subject. He was knowledgeable, calm, grandfatherly, and very reassuring that Katherine's BPD was treatable. He had a plan for meds and DBT therapy. Hope blossomed again for all of us. Driving two hours to Richmond once a month—a place I dislike immensely—was manageable. I was willing. I would try anything. Anything.

Within days of starting a new medication he recommended, she stopped it and disappeared. When she returned months later, she had run away from a boyfriend who had beaten and almost strangled her. She was pregnant. We went to see Dr. Freidel, and he was firm. "If you don't follow my recommendations, I cannot help you. You cannot keep this baby." He spoke of his long experience in this area. "I've seen too many tragic circumstances." Children neglected and abused. Mothers incapable of taking care of them. He said it was virtually impossible that she could be a mother. He referred to my daughter as "one of the most severe cases" he had ever seen.

She refused to ever go to Richmond to see him again. "He's given up on me" was her reason. "And I'm not giving up my baby."

CHAPTER SIX

Katherine, in Her Own Words: *"I am not my illness!"*

Shelters

In recent years I have been in and out of shelters. The few times I stayed in shelters in Virginia, I would get hit on by all kinds of creepy, mysterious men who would make me feel very uncomfortable and some who even wanted to help me get cigarettes in return for sexual favors. Some would take no for an answer. Some wouldn't.

The shelter that stands out the most clearly was the one I stayed at for more than a month in Haverhill, Massachusetts. It was called Mitch's Place, and it was one of those shelters that kicked you out at 7 a.m. bright and early, which in summer probably wasn't so bad, but when I was there it was the dead of winter. Given how small the town of Haverhill was, all the shelter people would run into each other all throughout the day. I met some of the most wonderful people there. Sure, just like any shelter, it had its fair share of crazies and drunks and drug addicts who I tended not to associate with, but for the most part it consisted of normal people just going through hardships, like job loss and whatnot. Some of the people I can say I became friends with because we were all in the same boat: broke and homeless, trying to survive and get on our feet. We'd help each other out, whether it be by sharing an extra jacket to stay warm or giving us a cigarette to bum because we ran out and couldn't afford to buy more. Everyone in my group of friends was my family. One old man who had suffered several strokes but was still going strong was the first person I met upon my arrival at Mitch's. Like myself, he was of Irish descent and like me, he had the Irish gift of gab, meaning we both talked a lot and more often than not annoyed the crap out of others. He told me his family built the ruin in Ireland known as Blarney Castle (where I have visited), which is a sacred stone castle with a stone that you can kiss if you bend back and is said to be blessed with good luck. I nicknamed him "Uncle Steve," and he was always a fun person to talk to, with words of wisdom and jokes he'd say in passing. I looked up to him as if he were family. Another friend, Michele, was like an aunt or a sister to me. She, too, suffered from borderline personality disorder and had one of her kids taken from her. She struggled to manage her illness just like me, so I always confided in her about the coping skills she had been practicing to deal with her own struggle. Every night at five o'clock my group of friends would meet in line in the mess hall, and then we'd all sit together and share jokes and stories about things that happened throughout the day.

Some shelters are worse than others, depending on the circumstances. However, living in a shelter could be looked at as a learning experience for someone like me, who was never raised in poverty, in shelters, or on the streets. I'll never forget it as long as I live. Whenever I see a homeless person on the street now, I'm reminded of when I lived that life, and my heart goes out to them. I learned that sometimes in life you have to fight to survive. Yes, fight, in this case to be able to stay warm, be safe, and have a full belly at the end of the day. In fact, sometimes things got so hard that I didn't want to wake up in the morning. But every time I felt that way, I would just keep pushing on and praying to God that things would get better.

Bullying

The bullying started in the fourth grade, but back then it was over petty stuff. The other girls called me ugly and made fun of me for the way I dressed and the fact that I wore glasses and braces. Even though my parents would always tell me I was beautiful, talented, and smart, I always felt it was only because they were my parents and they loved me, and as loving parents they would never say the things the kids at school were saying to me on a daily basis.

That part of my life, as hard as it was, was nothing compared to what I would deal with in the future. It was just the beginning.

By middle school, things got much worse. I didn't have a friend in the world, and I felt very insecure and began to really hate myself. All I wanted was a friend, but everyone seemed to hate me, and I could never understand why. Was I really so horrible that no one wanted to sit with me at lunch, let alone be friends with me?

This was around the time that I began to think about suicide. I thought to myself, "If I'm this bad, maybe one day I could end my pain and theirs if I just randomly disappeared."

By high school I had an even lower sense of self than I had before. Half the time people continued to act as if I were invisible, and the other half I was taunted at every turn. All I wanted to do was hide. Then I had my first boyfriend, and I thought finally someone would like me. But he broke up with me right after we had sex. He told everyone about it at school. He called me "stupid."

By early adulthood, my experience with others treating me badly reached its peak when I got my HIV diagnosis. Everything got progressively worse. I don't know how I got it, but I admit I lived a dangerous lifestyle that made it happen. Since my diagnosis I have been judged even more than ever before. I've lost friends. People sometimes wouldn't even hug me. Once the information got out, my whole life changed, both mentally and physically, and worst of all, socially. People gossiped about me and called me names.

As I look back, I realize that being treated badly by others, even well into my early adult life, has played a big part of my life and my mental illness.

Meds

Living with my illness has made me have to take all kinds of different meds and mood stabilizers through the course of my childhood, teen years, and early adult life, with most having little to almost no effect, or that had bad side effects, such as nausea, diarrhea, or tremors. It can be very upsetting for someone coping with mental illness to try different meds and therapies and have no positive result. Meds not appearing very effective can be so devastating and defeating when the individual wants nothing but to feel better and calmer, and to be able to have a somewhat normal life. It's very much trial and error when it comes to meds, but more often in my case I have had poor results, and this has been one of the most upsetting things in my daily life. A sufferer of mental illness wants a quick fix, and when it doesn't happen it can lead to great frustration, sometimes to the point where you might give up and refuse to continue taking them.

Being Sick

Every day I wake up and for the most part, feel lost. Sometimes I feel cursed to have mental problems and HIV, too. I blame myself and think that maybe it is somehow my fault, like in God's eyes I need to be punished for a reason unknown even to myself.

Sometimes my life and the way I see the world is a dark place that I cannot seem to pull myself out of. I feel sometimes as if the black hole keeps sucking me further and further down into a very dark world, like the underworld from Greek mythology, where nothing is there but hurt, pain, and suffering. Borderline Personality Disorder (BPD) is my version of the enemy known as Hades; I try to escape him and his wrath, his control over me, and sometimes I get close to being able to run free. Then he drags me down again. Every day I have to fight to remember that things are going to be tough and I have to keep carrying on and not let him beat me.

I just want to be normal. Sometimes I feel so misunderstood. People aren't the slightest bit patient; they think I act the way I do on purpose. Believe me, if I had a choice, I wouldn't act this way. It makes it hard to sustain friendships and hold jobs, and makes me feel like a worthless, disgusting person who never should have existed. When things get hard, the BPD voices in my head let ideas of suicide, cutting, taking drugs, or drinking myself till I die creep into my mind. Even in those bad times, I try my hardest to block out those thoughts.

All I want is to be able to live a normal life. Have a family, have a stable job that I'm good at, eventually go back to college and get a degree of some kind and use my illness to maybe help others in some way who feel as hopeless as I do much of the time. Having this illness should not make it impossible for me to enjoy life, fulfill my dreams, and live my life to the fullest.

When I am feeling strong I want to shout that my illness does not define me.

October 2013

CHAPTER SEVEN

Gossip and Judgments

*"If you are the parent of a child with a disability, you
are forever the parent of a disabled child; it is one of the
primary facts about you, fundamental to the way other
people perceive and decipher you."*

—ANDREW SOLOMON, *Far from the Tree*

Parents of emotionally disabled children may not always
be aware of it, but others who know their situation
begin to see them only in that context. Like cancer patients often
find, people withdraw, as if the condition is contagious. They
begin to see you as a martyr, a saint, someone to be pitied. It
is uncomfortable to be perceived this way, but you understand
that for many of those who know you, the perception grows
from sympathy.

Far more uncomfortable is to learn directly or indirectly
that people look at you in a not-so-sympathetic way; that some
cling to the idea that you brought your problems on yourself.

There are those who believe that you don't understand your child and they do. That you are not doing the right things to "fix" him. There may be rampant criticism and judgment (misjudgment) going on about you and your child among outsiders, even among professionals and others who are supposed to be helping.

How Could They? They Know Nothing

Dr. Laura Schlesinger, a conservative psychotherapist with a daily radio call-in program that reaches many millions of listeners, regularly blames dysfunctional kids on parents. She is especially accusatory and harsh when she speaks to divorced parents, single moms, and working mothers. She has stated unequivocally that leaving a child in the care of babysitters, nannies, and daycare constitutes "child neglect." She is so wrong. While she has quick answers to parents about how their lifestyle choices have harmed their children, you will not hear her take a call from a parent who follows her advice for excellent parenthood but still has a disturbed child.

* * *

Emily, a stay-at-home suburban mother in Maryland, describes the pain of learning that her eighth-grade son Matt had a bad reputation in the neighborhood. "I was shocked when I learned that the guy who managed the neighborhood pool in the summer—a parent and teacher himself—was gabbing around the pool to other parents that mine was a bad kid, a 'gang leader'." Emily was well aware that her son was no choir-boy, and she was dealing with some difficult issues with him, but this man's two sons were hanging out with Matt doing the same kinds of teenage pranks and troublemaking; in fact, they were egging Matt on to some risky behaviors. Emily says, "At one point I called to give him a heads up about what our kids were doing. He didn't want to hear about it, didn't believe it, or blamed my son for all of it." He advised her to "Keep your kid away from mine." Matt later told her that one day when this man was mowing his lawn, Matt happened to be walking toward his house. This man turned off his mower and stared, saying, "Keep walking, kid." Emily says, "How could he? What kind of person—a parent and a teacher, no less—could treat a neighbor and friend of his sons that way?"

* * *

In the wake of what occurred in Newtown, Connecticut, Liza Long, mother of a disturbed boy in Boise, Idaho, wrote "I am Adam Lanza's Mother" describing similar difficulties with her thirteen-year-old son. She wrote about the doctors, the medications, the stigma, and the failures of the mental health system. To heal from the horror of Newtown, she wrote of the need for "a meaningful, nationwide conversation about mental health." Many were outraged by the frankness of her post, and she was attacked about "… her parenting and . . . her decision to go public with her child's mental illness." In my view, their judgments only reinforce the stigma and allow others to continue to distance themselves from the problem of mentally ill children and the isolation of their parents trying to help them.

* * *

We did much to help Brendan from the time he first exhibited anxiety and school difficulty in elementary school: doctors, psychiatrists, medications, tutors. He grew into a troubled teen, failing in school, sneaking out at night, smoking and drinking. Outpatient treatment was not helping; in fact, he often would disappear when it came time to go to appointments. One summer when he was seventeen, he disappeared the day our family was to leave for our annual vacation in New England. We left anyway. A few days later, a neighbor who was watching our house called to tell us a large group of loud teenagers was partying in our back yard. We called the police, who broke up the party and arrested our son and several of his friends for underage drinking and marijuana possession. The parents of the others quickly got their kids out of jail the next day, but we refused to come for Brendan, asking that he be kept in juvenile hall to ensure his safety while we had the time to arrange through a lawyer for him to be court-ordered to a treatment facility out of state. Brendan's court-appointed lawyer didn't hide her disapproval of what we had done. "What is wrong with you people? Most parents want their kids OUT of juvie," She sniffed. Even the judge made clear his contempt for the situation and our arrangements for our son to be sentenced and taken directly to treatment. "Whose bright idea was all this?" he asked from the bench, and we had to raise our hands.

Family Members
Make Judgments, Too

My own father told me more than once to give up on Brendan. "Invest in the good ones, you are wasting time and money on a lost cause." No matter how often I explained the ways in which I was not neglecting my three other children, he was unconvinced. His easy dismissal of my troubled boy—his grandson—whom I loved so much, broke my heart. Give up on my son? Never. Further, his own misunderstanding of the situation belied the fact that he himself had once been a troubled high school dropout due to emotional and family problems, and had returned to high school at age eighteen to finish. He went on to obtain two undergraduate and two graduate degrees, and had a long and successful career.

When Katherine was little, my mother-in-law attributed all of Katherine's behavior problems to her being "spoiled." It did no good for my husband or me to explain about emotional and learning disabilities in children; she could not "sit" with Katherine's problems without blaming someone. Ironically, she and other members of her own family had varying levels of unhealthy psychological symptoms which looked like a genetic link to Katherine: arguing, lying, manipulating, blaming others, paranoia, one-upmanship, suspicion, criticism, and misanthropy raised to the level of art. One of her sisters had been hospitalized more than once for bipolar disorder. But that generation, born in the early decades of the twentieth century, could not conceive of or discuss the taboo of mental illness in their own family. The stigma was tightly controlled by a wall of denial, punctuated by behind-the-scenes gossip and criticism.

Professionals Who Should Know Better

Professionals who devote their work life to emotionally or learning disabled children can also exhibit misunderstanding and judgmentalism.

When Katherine returned from twenty months in the therapeutic wilderness school, she was in good physical and mental health and ready to resume a normal high school experience to get her diploma. Almost eighteen, she had fallen far behind her neighborhood school classmates and didn't want the embarrassment of returning there. We requested that her Individual Education Plan (IEP) place her in the center for emotional disabilities (ED) at another school. This turned out to be a huge mistake. She spent that year enduring abuse by other students in the ED center, while her own behaviors became worse. The following year, we formally requested that her IEP return her to her home school. In the meeting where we were supposed to consider, discuss, and determine the best response to this reasonable request, it was clear that the people from the ED center and the home school director had conferred and decided ahead of time to dismiss our pleas for help. Katherine had come to be judged a problem child, and her home school didn't want her back. They had given up on her. We could not let her return to that awful situation, so we were forced to file a formal IEP disagreement and remove her from the school system. We never heard from the county again.

We were running out of options. She was nineteen, with barely a sophomore level of education. She wanted to quit school altogether, but we fought her on that and enrolled her in a private tutoring program to finish her high school coursework. The program was a step up from homeschooling and was run by an experienced and highly educated woman whose own children had suffered problems in school. Despite her experience and knowledge, she was judgmental about Katherine, as well. She informed us that the only problem with our daughter was that our public school system (which has a reputation as one of the best in the country) was incompetent in testing, screening, and teaching children. This "expert" couldn't accept that our daughter had learning issues and emotional disabilities that led to school avoidance because of social problems and academic failure. By the time we had invested many thousands of dollars in her program and finally parted ways, Katherine had spent almost two years continuing to struggle academically and avoiding classes because of the same sorts of emotional problems. She got a diploma, but she was not educated. The program director gave every indication that she still believed Katherine's problems were a result of incompetent schooling, but now she also seemed to blame poor parenting on our part, as well.

How Could They? They Know Nothing (Part 2: Because They Don't Want to Know)

Why are people so judgmental?

The slaughter at Sandy Hook Elementary School in

December 2012 was so inconceivable that, to reduce our horror and anxiety, we need to explain, blame, and try to make some kind of sense of the inexplicable. It is beyond the logic of human beings to fathom what went on in Adam Lanza's brain that could drive him to do such an abominable act. But still, we feel compelled to try.

And so, people blame the mother. It is easy to judge Nancy Lanza, who allowed her disturbed son to have access to guns and training on how to use them; the mother who has been described as having accommodated Adam's every whim. Perhaps she was dealing with overwhelming fear of what her son might be capable of if she said "no." She had "spent the years when her son Adam was between nine and seventeen consumed by the search to help cure his affliction." This mother had all the "resources to see any doctor in the state, but by 2008 she told a friend that finding adequate treatment for her son had become 'a lost cause'." (Andrew Solomon, *Far from the Tree*)

My experience tells me that she deserves sympathy, not judgment. We can't know what she understood about her son's mind. Being the mother, we expect she knew him best. Chances are she didn't know her son at all.

It's been said in what is actually a humorous but brutal truth that "insanity is inherited; you get it from your children." I concur. My own behaviors could be judged and criticized as crazy, ineffective, or even making things worse, so in my way I understand and grieve for Nancy Lanza. I have given in to a disturbed child too often when I believed in some superficial indication of change, only to be blindsided by more horrifying behavior. I have locked myself in the bathroom to avoid a screaming kid banging on the door. I have given in to the demands of a disturbed child, driven by fear of a raging tantrum, verbal abuse, or even physical attack. I have been known to lock my bedroom door for the night out of fear of being awakened in the dark by an unpredictable and possibly dangerous approach from my child. It is important to say that my children were never violent, yet I didn't understand them and couldn't stake my life on what they were capable of. At times I collected the knives in my kitchen and hid them from view. When things seemed to improve, the knives were brought out again and the bedroom door unlocked, but I had to return to those precautions when things went sour again in the cyclical way that mental illness proceeds.

* * *

After he killed six people and injured thirteen others at the University of California in Santa Barbara in May of 2014, Elliot Rodger's father, Peter, established a website where the public can share comments and their own stories. It was started with Peter's story about his mentally ill son and coordinated with a television interview with Barbara Walters in which Peter describes how little he understood about his son. On the website, while there were many supportive and sympathetic comments posted, others were cruelly judgmental. Some comments included:

» "… with Elliott, the signs were there that something was VERY WRONG. From reading his 'manifesto,' that only strengthens the theory that you were an absentee father.

I am not trying to be cruel, but it is important to get the message out to parents that they need to be active in their children's lives. While you were out chasing dreams of being a Hollywood director, flying all over the world, your son was sitting home alone, stewing in his own mental health issues."

»   "Peter Rodger said that his son 'hid' his sickness from his parents. How could that be? The kid was seeing a psychiatrist FROM THE AGE OF EIGHT, for Christssake! The mother told the psychiatrist NOT to call the police if it seemed that Elliot was heading in a very troubling direction, but to call her (the mother) instead. It was obvious that the kid was totally off-the-wall from early on."

* * *

"Humans, as a rule, don't like mad people unless they are good at painting, and only then once they are dead. . . . Basically, the key rule is, if you want to appear sane on Earth you have to be in the right place, wearing the right clothes, saying the right things, and only stepping on the right kind of grass."

—MATT HAIG, *The Humans*

Judgment Often Proves So Wrong

I admit it. I can be judgmental, too.

My sister raised her children in a way I often judged to be wrong. She allowed her kids to see graphic war movies and other R-rated productions from the time they were very young.

As teens they were given cars, lots of freedom, and few rules. The family has a serious love affair with guns. They have an arsenal in their home, and they frequent the shooting range. These kids have grown up to be impressive and accomplished young people: brilliant, polite, witty, outstanding students, ambitious, fearless, adventurous, accomplished, and happy.

My brother and his wife seem to have by all outward appearances a perfect home, marriage, and children. They have said they were raising their children in a "Christ-centered home," implying that if a family has problems or the children don't turn out right, well, it must be they aren't Christ-centered enough. These parents were clear about how they were never away from their children, implying that it was not acceptable for working parents to engage day care or have evenings out with the service of a babysitter or travel and leave children with grandparents. While I judged their simplistic and overprotective approach might cause their children damage, I was wrong. My nieces and nephew have grown up to be amazing young adults now: healthy and fit, wholesome, religious, calm, smart, polite, and hardworking.

Lots of families have children turn out well. Do we credit parenting, or DNA? Too often the credit goes to the parents, when it might just be random luck of good genes.

Compassion, Not Judgment

Wisdom has come to me with knowledge and experience. In the past, I looked at other families and questioned all the things I thought they were doing wrong, or looked at myself and tried to pinpoint what I must have done wrong. It is true that "compare leads to despair." Now I know that the problems of disturbed children do not arise from watching violent movies—or protecting children from them. Nor do they arise from taking them to church, or not, or skipping grace at the family dinner table, or any other of the infinite number of influences on a child's development.

In so many ways, the outcome of one's job as a parent is only as controllable and predictable as a roll of the dice, the arbitrariness of the universe, the random combination of genes, or dumb luck. Parenting certainly contributes to the outcome, but it is still unknown how much. We certainly know that parenting is not the ultimate influence that determines it. Thus, no one is in the right to judge, gossip, shame, or blame either a child or his parents or his caregivers for mental illness. No one outside a family can really understand what that family is dealing with, or the actions they have taken to help their situation. So, to be blunt, unless you want to offer help to a family that is suffering, shut the hell up.

If your child is perfect, you are lucky. Please show compassion for family of the child who is not.

CHAPTER EIGHT

Mental Illness Affects Us All

*"... few people who have not experienced it up close
buy the idea of a behavioral disease. It has the ring
of an excuse, a license for self-absorption on the most
extreme scale. It suggests that one chooses madness
and not the other way around." (86)*

MICHAEL GREENBERG, *Hurry Down Sunshine*

ental illness only gets the spotlight when something horrible happens. Then, in short order, the spotlight fades, and people turn their attention to other things. We ignore the illness because we think it only happens to other people. Yet, if we are honest with ourselves, we *fear* it is happening to us, or people close to us. Haven't we all had a situation where we write someone off as "he's just nuts." Or we stop visiting Aunt Gertrude to avoid her "eccentricities." Or change jobs because the boss "is a psycho." Or blame ourselves to excuse a loved one's abuse? This must stop. Our society must face the facts and stop living in denial that brain disease only happens somewhere else, to someone else. It affects us all.

The fact is, one in four of us will suffer from our own, or another's, mental illness.

Not a Lifestyle Choice

Mental illness is defined by the National Alliance for the Mentally Ill (NAMI) as "a medical condition that disrupts a person's thinking, feeling, mood, ability to relate to others and daily functioning." It is a medical condition, not a lifestyle choice. In fact, it takes choices away.

Think for a moment on the scary thought in the following online post, a few days following a great actor's death from addiction:

> "Phillip Seymour Hoffman did not have choice or free will and neither do you. . . . What we have on our hands in the U.S. is a mental health, i.e., brain health, crisis . . . And even though we have had great breakthroughs in neuroscience, we are woefully lagging behind in treating people who suffer and offering support to their families . . . How did this happen? There are more than a few ways to answer that question. One of the important answers is that we are naturally defensive against the idea that brain disorders —which disconnect us from our free will—exist. It's too frightening an idea to consider."
>
> —Debbie Bayer, MA, MFTI, blog

And this, in response to Robin Williams' suicide:

"Suicidal depression is like having to sneeze. The impulse can be so strong, that you simply follow your body's command without thinking too much of it. You don't think about your family or the reasons not to do it. All you're feeling is an incredible itch to sneeze, and you're certain that anything short of sneezing wouldn't relieve you of the sensation".

—Therese Borchard

Set aside your denial and read the following words of Dr. Edwin Torrey, a specialist in the area of mental health and author of *The Invisible Plague*:

"Imagine ... an epidemic that begins not over a few weeks or a few years but over a few decades. Imagine an epidemic that does not cause cupsful of sputum, skin cancers, or a 60-pound weight loss, but rather affects the brain, causing people to have strange beliefs, extreme mood swings, and illogical thinking, to hear voices that others cannot hear, and to exhibit bizarre behavior in response to their strange beliefs and illogical thinking. Imagine an epidemic that does not quickly kill a large percentage of those affected, but instead slowly kills 15 percent by suicide. Imagine an epidemic that is so insidious and ingratiating that, two centuries after it has begun, it is barely noticed, so blended into the fabric of people's lives that a few otherwise intelligent people even deny that the disease exists. Imagine an epidemic that affects over 4 million Americans, most of them in the prime of their lives, and will continue to affect more than one every one hundred people born, but that is not recognized as a major public health problem and is largely ignored by officials overseeing the nation's health."

Shootings and Other Crimes

After decades of hiding crazy in the attic, the recent horrors of Phoenix, Aurora, Sandy Hook, and too many other places have slapped us in the face with what mental illness, improperly treated, can wreak. In the last few years, it seems every week there is another random shooting by a mentally unbalanced person. Often, when this happens, we learn in 20-20 hindsight that the person was hearing voices or making suicidal comments, and that there were people who knew. *There were people who knew.* How do we cope? We pass the blame for not heeding the signs and preventing the violence.

Despite all the attention to the violence committed by sick people, a mentally ill person is more likely to be victim of crime than a perpetrator. While the sensationalism makes it appear that there are millions of crazies out there with guns, that is an unfair impression and promotes the stigma about the mentally ill. If we better understand that mentally ill people are fragile and vulnerable, it might finally make it possible that the needed changes could come.

It starts with treatment. Sometimes that means that people who are ill might need to be confined for the protection of themselves and others. It is nearly impossible in most states to forcibly commit a loved one into treatment, and even if one could force it, where are the beds? In the case of Creigh Deeds, tragedy could have been averted had there been a place for his son, Gus. Imagine for a moment the horror of being attacked by your beloved child, and even while he is trying to kill you, you understand that he is not in his right mind. You have done what you could to get him the help he needs. But today, while you are being attacked, the help isn't there. As you recover from your injuries, you have to make his funeral arrangements.

When we talk about crime, consider the following. When it was decided in the late 1960s and 70s to free mental patients from the confines of mental hospitals, a policy benignly referred to as "deinstitutionalization," the idea was to spare them the suffering they were enduring in what amounted to warehouses for disabled human beings. They were caged and abused like animals. That was a crime. That crime has, over time, been compounded: The unintended consequences of closing down the hospitals and giving the mentally ill freedom was that it left them with nowhere to go.

Left on their own, in a world they often can't navigate, their eccentric behaviors and bad decisions often lead them to run afoul of the law. It is estimated that there might be some 930,000 mentally ill people in the United States, but only some 55,000 are in hospitals. Where are the rest? Too many mental patients are once again being warehoused, this time in prisons, the new asylums. That, too, is a crime. Most don't need incarceration; they need humane and effective treatment, a decent place to live, and enough supervision to guide them.

* * *

My daughter has skirted the edges of the law for years, with relatively small infractions such as shoplifting and minor drug use. However, what horrifies me is that she has been a victim of serious crime more than once: She has endured rape, beatings, and theft. She is a sweet girl with an open heart, but because she has learning disabilities and an anxiety disorder and has such a fragile and flexible sense of self, she has made choices that have put her repeatedly in harm's way. One boyfriend tried to choke her to death. Another held her at gunpoint until the police intervened. Another beat her and threatened her and her family if she told anyone. Only when he broke her arm did it come to light.

More than once we have had to help her to change her address, her name, and her cell phone number in an effort to run and hide from the scary people in her life. Because of her lowlife associates and years of instability, we took her key to our house away and installed an alarm system. We have paid for her to stay in hotels and apartments in a mostly failed effort to separate her from "bad people" and to keep those people away from our home. If I didn't have two protective dogs, I would live in fear of these people tracking us down. I worry every day that a past bad boyfriend will track her down and do her harm. *Lifetime* movie, anyone?

The worst crime that has been inflicted on my daughter is she has been a willing target for predatory males, and I consider every one who ever had sex with her to be a rapist. The ones who gave her drugs and encouraged her cigarette smoking have damaged her health in ways tantamount to parental abuse of a child. The biggest crime perpetrated against her is her HIV infection.

Somebody passed a lethal illness on to her. She doesn't know who, but she will have to live with the disease, a daily cocktail of medications, and the knowledge of her role in contracting it, for the rest of her life. Though good treatments make HIV no longer the death sentence it used to be, she is a young person who lives every day knowing that she could be one illness away from the grave. It threatens everything important about her future: her ability to hold a job, her ability to have a healthy romantic relationship, her ability to parent.

Mental Illness Affects Our Communities and Our Pockets

Even those who haven't got mental illness in the family are still paying for it. Consider the following costs:

» "The massacre at Virginia Tech—besides taking 32 lives and permanently scarring hundreds more—cost taxpayers about $48.2 million. That's according to the Center for American Progress, a liberal D.C. think tank that analyzed Cho's April 16, 2007, attack by sifting through the legal bills, university staffing costs, police costs, hospital bills and autopsy receipts" (Petula Dvorak, *Washington Post*).

» "In the last twenty years, taxpayers have funded increasing amounts of disability payments to the growing numbers of people becoming eligible because of mental illness. Every day 1,100 adults and children are added to the government disability rolls because they have become newly disabled by mental illness." NAMI estimates the cost of untreated mental illness is $100 billion dollars per year in the United States.

» Approximately 57.7 million Americans-experience a mental health disorder in a given year. Prior to the passing of the Affordable Care Act, which requires insurance companies to cover mental health services, the federal government reported that 25 percent of uninsured adults have a mental health condition or substance use disorder or both.

We all have an interest in improving our mental health system. Today, homeless schizophrenics wander the streets, talking to their hallucinations and defecating in the bushes, because there are no hospitals or group homes where they can live like human beings. Laws devised to help them have made it impossible for their families to force them into those nonexistent homes anyway. People walk by and pretend they don't see. Is this the kind of world we want to live in? Are we our brother's keeper? Yes. Because most of us do care, and most of us see this as a blight on the landscape of the richest country in the world.

Not only that. We must face what we know: Someone you know is dealing with mental or emotional illness in the family right now. The next person murdered in a public shooting might be your mother, your brother, your daughter. The family living on your street that is the source of rumors you ignore may turn out to be the one that shocks you. "I didn't know she was capable of such a thing!" "He seemed so quiet." "Sure there were some signs, but we never dreamed—!"

Trust me on this: Don't assume that the mentally ill street person has no one who cares. Somewhere there are people who love him—a parent, child, spouse, ex-spouse, or friend—people who have tried everything, who time and again have given up, only to try one more time. They wonder where and how their sick relative is. Is she in a shelter with good people caring for her? Is he living under a bridge? Did she eat today? Has he found a way to stay sober, to get and keep a job, to live a decent life? Is she hooking, drugging, shoplifting? If they could know that a passerby took a second look, took a moment to offer a bit of help, they would experience a tiny bit of hope.

The story of Ted Williams, the homeless man with a crack addiction and the golden voice of the successful DJ he once was, is an example. The world stopped walking by. It was a rocky transition for him, but he sobered up, was hired at a job using his talent, had a home, and began repairing his family relationships.

Even Children Can Be Mentally Ill

Therese Borchard calls it *"Fourth-Grade Syndrome* because that's the year I remember as being disabled by depression. I felt uncomfortable in my skin, like a kind of hostage in a cruel and ugly world. At one point in the year, I couldn't stop crying for a week and remember my mom not knowing whether or not she should take me to the hospital. I constantly begged God to take me and let me live with Him and the saints."

* * *

Tricia took her teenage daughter Anna to see a psychiatrist when depression seemed to paralyze her and she talked of suicide.

This mother tells of the painful moment when she realized that Anna needed help: "We were looking through old photographs from a happy family vacation we had taken years before, when Anna was about 8. There we all were, three girls and their parents, smiling on a beach. Such a happy time, I thought. Anna looked at the photo, and sighed wistfully, 'I remember that picture. I felt so sad that day because I knew that no one in the world loved me'." Tears appear in Tricia's eyes when she tells this story. She raises her hand to her heart. "I'm her mom! She has always been loved! How could she ever come to feel that way, and how could I not have known how she felt?"

* * *

We now know that mental illness can emerge sooner than was previously understood. It used to be that only adults could be diagnosed, but in recent decades experts have recognized that symptoms can be traced back to childhood. In fact, according to the National Institutes of Health, mental illness is "not uncommon among children and adolescents..."

» Less than one-third of the children under age eighteen who have a serious mental health problem receive any mental health services.

» As many as 1 in every 33 children may be depressed. Depression in adolescents may be as high as 1 in 8.

» Suicide is the third leading cause of death for 15- to 24-year-olds and the sixth leading cause of death for 5- to

15-year-olds.

» Schizophrenia is rare in children under age 12, but it occurs in about 3 of every 1,000 adolescents.

» Between 118,700 and 186,600 youths in the juvenile justice system have at least one mental illness.

» Of the 100,000 teenagers in juvenile detention, an estimated 60 percent have behavioral, cognitive, or emotional problems.

Often, adults who seek treatment for alcoholism or drug addiction can tell of their first high or drunk happening in middle school, or even earlier. They remember it being the first time they "felt better." Later, as adults, if they get treatment, they recognize it was the start of self-medicating to escape from anxiety, fear, depression, or other mental pain.

Suffering Spills Over

"When another person makes you suffer, it is because he suffers
deeply within himself, and his suffering is spilling over.
He does not need punishment; he needs help. That's the
message he is sending."

ZEN BUDDHIST MASTER THICH NHAT HANH

In his article, "The Reckoning," published in the March 2014 issue of *The New Yorker*, Andrew Solomon describes the inner turmoil and difficult history that drove Adam Lanza toward that awful day in December 2012. It is a story that parallels in many ways the stories of other mass shooters, such as Seung-Hui Cho, Michael Carneal, and Elliott Rodger. Lanza had a brain disorder, which made him an outcast at home and in school. Like many troubled young men, especially those who attack, he had an inner life that others could not see, and he turned to violent videogames and hate-filled Internet websites, while compiling and hiding an arsenal.

Park Dietz, a psychiatrist who, in 1986, coined the term "pseudocommando," says that "preoccupation with weapons and war regalia makes up for a sense of impotence and failure." Self-loathing grows, and so does hatred for everyone else. James Knoll, a forensic psychiatrist at The State University of New York (SUNY), has written that Adam's act conveyed a message: "I carry profound hurt—I'll go ballistic and transfer it onto you."

These people are sick. Society unfairly expects their parents to be their doctors and to understand what is going in inside their minds. Mentally ill people do not belong on the street, nor should they be locked up in penitentiaries. They should not be wandering through life unnoticed until something terrible happens. Most of all, no matter what the most political view is, we can all agree that they should not have access to guns or other weapons. They belong in a supervised and safe care facility where they can get the professional medical treatment that may allow them to create some kind of stable independent life, bearing in mind that mental illness can be treated, but usually not cured. Such facilities barely exist in this country, and the need is massive and growing.

And whose responsibility is it? Look at the pictures of the children killed at Sandy Hook Elementary School and you will know the answer.

It Takes a Village

It is true that it takes a village to raise a child. This is not some hippie socialist idea about communes, state daycare, and sister wives. It doesn't have to mean we are responsible for other people's children, nor is it a license to stick one's nose into other families' business, but it does mean that our community does affect how a child develops. As stated earlier, parents have limited control over how their child becomes himself. In part this is due to the pervasiveness of outside influences. Teachers, babysitters, coaches, clergy, peers, other parents—all carry some weight that affect a child's growth. Parenting classes, teacher training, and school health curricula should include the latest information from the mental health field and the actions that can be taken. Even children on the playground could benefit from age-appropriate knowledge. Middle school is not too early to understand what "if you see something, say something" could mean in this context. A program about mental health could be useful and help sidetrack the tendency to bully or tease another student who seems different. We all should have some knowledge about early signs of emotional disturbance so that efforts at intervention can be supported. We all should keep up with the research into new and better treatments for the youngest of our mentally ill.

Susan Klebold, mother of the Columbine shooter Dylan Klebold, has written a memoir of the horror that she experienced: *A Mother's Reckoning: Living in the Aftermath of Tragedy* (2016). She writes of how their family was ordinary, their child seemingly "normal." If they were there, she missed the signs of Dylan's disturbed thinking, depression, and suicidality. Among the things she has come to understand in the wake of this terrible event is that we all should understand more about brain disease:

> "We teach our kids the importance of good dental care, proper nutrition, and financial responsibility. How many of us teach our children to monitor their own brain health, or know how to do it ourselves?"

This must happen before these children's illnesses worsen due to their experiences of becoming outcasts and the targets of bullies, or simply growing up with silent, invisible pain that may find a terrible outlet. Think of a child who is viewed as "odd" in elementary school; this can lead to an ever-growing and deepening reaction, as the child feels rejected by peers, teachers, or family members. The child may then react in even more odd ways, leading to more misunderstandings between him and others, eventually warping his ability to grow up in a healthy way. If the "village" has some understanding about this at the outset and engages in positive approaches, a child who is perceived as "different" has a better chance of embracing instead of running from his uniqueness.

The Upside of Crazy

"Our hospital was famous and housed many great poets and singers. Did the hospital specialize in poets and singers or was it that poets and singers specialized in madness?"

—SUSANNA KAYSEN, *Girl, Interrupted*

Set aside the horrific tragedies that can happen. What do we as a society lose if we allow a percentage of our population to endure lives with no meaning, no purpose, no contribution? History tells us that some of the greatest people who have walked this earth had psychological issues ranging from depression to anxiety to bipolar disorder to substance abuse. The National Alliance for Mental Illness (NAMI) rightly states that people with mental illness enrich our lives. They come from all walks of life, and some of them have recognizable names: political leaders such as Abraham Lincoln, Winston Churchill, and Theodore Roosevelt; journalists such as Mike Wallace and Jane Pauley; social activists such as Abbie Hoffman and Dorothy Day; scientists and mathematicians such as Isaac Newton and John Nash (of *A Beautiful Mind.);* business leaders such as Ted Turner.

Kay Redfield Jamison, of the prestigious Johns Hopkins department of psychiatry and one of the nation's pre-eminent experts in the study of bipolar illness, is bipolar herself. She has said that, "There are a lot of studies that suggest a higher rate of creativity in bipolars than the general population." This is borne out by the musical genius of Thelonius Monk, Wolfgang Amadeus Mozart, Ludwig von Beethoven, Billy Joel, and Kurt Cobain; actors such as Robin Williams, Brooke Shields, Vivien Leigh, and Phillip Seymour Hoffman; the literary talent of Virginia Woolf, Ernest Hemingway, William Styron, Sylvia Plath, Edgar Allan Poe, Charles Dickens, Philip K. Dick, and Eugene O'Neill; artists Jackson Pollock and Vincent Van Gogh.

Marsha Linehan, who has been known for years worldwide for developing the dialectical behavioral therapy (DBT) for borderline personality disorder (BPD), only recently revealed that she had suffered from BPD herself and had "a history of self-mutilation and suicidality." She explained how, when she was twenty years old, psychiatrists at the institution where she was hospitalized for over two years declared her as "one of the most disturbed patients in the hospital." Had she not survived her own mental illness, the field would not now have a proven treatment for BPD, an illness that was previously deemed untreatable.

All of these, and others, have contributed and enriched our society in immeasurable ways. It may be true that genius and madness are close relatives, but look what these people have contributed to the world. How many more have been missed? How many are out there now, languishing in prisons or dying on the street?

After his penetrating 2013 interview with Ted Williams, the homeless man with the golden voice, Dr. Phil McGraw spoke of his hope for Williams. He added, "This makes me wonder: How many human resources are we wasting on the streets today?"

Indeed. How many are still in middle school heading down a worrisome path, with parents in isolation and despair, in the dark as to what to do?

William Styron, author of *Sophie's Choice* and *The Confessions of Nat Turner*, chronicled his late-in-life bout with suicidal depression in his book *Darkness Visible: A Memoir of Madness.* He writes that he came to understand his seeming sudden illness had, in fact, its origins in his childhood: a father who had been hospitalized for depression, but even more affecting, the death of his mother when he was thirteen. " . . . depression, when it finally came to me, was in fact no stranger, not even a visitor totally unannounced; it had been tapping at my door for decades." It is important to note that he survived his illness, and in an effort to share the hope for others, eloquently compared his experience to Dante's poetic descent into the abyss, and his returning ascent upward into "the shining world":

> *In the middle of the journey of our life*
> *I found myself in a dark wood,*
> *For I had lost the right path. ...*
> *And so we came forth, and once again beheld the stars.*

* * *

My daughter has BPD. She is also a talented singer and sketch artist. She has a knack for design; she dreams of being a window dresser or fashion designer or hair stylist. She maintains that her illness does not define her. She is more than a "case."

She has aspirations beyond today. She has not given up. The rest of us should not give up, either.

* * *

*"Here's to the crazy ones. The misfits. The rebels.
The troublemakers. The round pegs in the square holes.
The ones who see things differently. They're not fond of rules.
And they have no respect for the status quo. You can quote
them, disagree with them, glorify or vilify them.
About the only thing you can't do is ignore them.
Because they change things. They push the human race
forward. And while some may see them as the crazy ones,
we see genius. Because the people who are crazy enough
to think they can change the world, are the ones who do."*

—STEVE JOBS, APPLE INC.

CHAPTER NINE

Working with the Helping Professions

How can you know if your child is mentally ill? Is there a guidebook? Sadly, no. But parents usually know when the time has arrived that a professional must be consulted. Frequently, in hindsight, a parent may admit that there were times they wondered if something must be done, but it didn't happen until they faced a situation with their child that seemed so far out of the norm it was inescapable, or they got the comment of a teacher, or a coach, or another parent that indicated, "Something's not right here."

* * *

Dee Smith's little boy Andrew was high-energy, talkative, high-strung, and easily frustrated. His reactions had progressed from screaming toddler tantrums to tearing his room apart to punching a hole in the bedroom wall to finally the day he raised his fist and hit his mother in a fit of temper. For Dee, that was the last straw: It was time for professional help. Andrew had his first meeting with a psychotherapist on his eighth birthday.

* * *

Helen knew by the time her daughter was two that something wasn't right. It wasn't anything dramatic or specific, just a feeling that her child was "different." She and her husband had adopted Erin right after birth, and she was their only child. Helen kept thinking it was just that she was a new mother, inexperienced, overthinking everything. She asked another mom, a friend, "How do you know if something is wrong with your child?" and her friend's answer was, "That you are asking yourself that question says it all, doesn't it?" By the time Erin was four, she was in the care of specialists, and this began years of therapies, diagnoses, medications, and the nightmare of mental illness.

* * *

When my daughter Katherine was two, her constant talking and inattentive mobility made her accident prone. I had to constantly catch her from major falls and bumping into things. When she was crawling at around age ten months, she suffered a bump on the head that left a scar. Then she broke an arm at age two and broke the other one at age three. After she learned how to climb (fall) out of her crib, we had to lock her in her bedroom at night for fear of her tumbling down the hallway stairs in the dark. I was convinced she had Attention Deficit Hyperactivity Disorder (ADHD). Her pediatrician said he prescribed ADHD medication at that young age only if the parents were demanding it because their kid was driving them nuts. By the time she was three, I was there.

When It is Time for Professional Help

By the time a parent and child arrive for the first appointment with a treatment professional, they have already been through hell with their child, followed by a nightmare of trying to find the right kind of help. And this is just the beginning. There is hurt, disappointment, frustration, anger, fear, and more. They need information and truth, but they also want hope. They want to know it is a passing phase.

The so-called "helping professions" might more accurately be called the "sorta-helping" professions. It is a line of work that may initially satisfy an altruistic desire to help people, but that goal has a number of obstacles that are thorns on the rosebush:

- » Psychiatric treatment is expensive. For too many families, it is not an option.

- » Treatment professionals often won't take insurance.

- » Families with insurance must still navigate through constant denial and obstruction of benefits and reimbursements.

» Treatment professionals are not available nights and week-ends, and it seems that is when each crisis occurs.

» Psychology is a frustratingly inexact science. Outcomes are often not measurable, and each case is molded by unique characteristics of each child and family.

People don't choose to be mentally ill. Parents don't cause it, and they cannot cure it. It can, however, be treated. If oncologists can go to work every day knowing they face a high failure rate, then mental health professionals should be able to face and make clear to families that mental illness is entirely different from many physical illnesses where there are usually clear protocols that match clear symptoms. Even realizing this, too many professionals want to prescribe a "one size fits all" approach to treating a troubled child. Snap diagnosis judgments become the norm, with no consultation with previous professionals. Vague ideas about this or that possible diagnosis or combination of conditions are tossed around like dice. It is rare to roll snake eyes.

Parents are desperate for a definitive conclusion, a fail-safe plan to make the problems go away and make their child's life "normal." When the child is young, hope blooms constant that in growing up the problems will surely disappear, and in the meantime, medications and counseling must suffice. This is the life ring a parent hangs onto while waiting for that expected rescue ship of maturity.

As years go by and things don't get better, or even get worse, hope fades. All the dreams of sending him to Princeton, or seeing her on the Broadway stage, devolve downward. The goal of college becomes that of a high school diploma; then the goal becomes keeping her from dropping out and running away, then it becomes keeping him out of jail, then keeping her safe from harm. Finally the dream is just to keep him breathing. "If I can just keep him alive until he grows out of this!" It is a tough moment when the parent finally sees the brick wall with giant graffiti letters that say "ILLNESS" written all over it. This problem is here to stay; it can't be wished or prayed away.

What's left? The flaws of the mental health system.

Katherine's Experience

A diverse army of professionals has been part of my daughter's life beginning at age three, when her preschool teacher informed us that "something's not right." From that moment on, she has encountered literally dozens of "experts." My closest count is about thirty-five different teachers, special educators, doctors, psychiatrists, social workers, child development experts, testing professionals, education consultants, occupational therapists and counselors, all of whom provided different suggestions and guidance about diagnosis, treatments, programs, prescriptions, and various combinations of those. Who were we to believe? Who could we trust and rely on to help us chart a path to help her?

At countless meetings I was informed that the bright light of my life, my only daughter, a little girl with the dimples and shiny hair whom I thought of as cute, talkative, smart, charming, and charismatic, instead "presented well," but was in reality someone I didn't recognize. She was:

» attention deficient

» "almost retarded"

» bipolar (rapid-cycling type)

» perceptually disabled—"almost like a blind person"

» a case of pervasive developmental delay

» suffering from nonverbal learning disabilities

» "on the spectrum," a possible Asperger's syndrome case

» possibly brain damaged

» a "severe" case of borderline personality disorder

» a clear case of PTSD

» possessing a frontal lobe with "no brakes"

Of all the professionals we have consulted, only one stayed with us for more than a short time. David Mason, LPC, worked with our family for more than a decade. He is no magician, but he is a caring, devoted counselor who often went beyond the call of duty to help our family. He never undermined our determination or hope, promising our family early on "I will never abandon you," when all the other treatment professionals eventually gave up or referred us to others. He never gave us the message that my child is no more than a case that can't be solved.

To those who gave up on us, I would say: My child is my treasure. You don't know her as I do. You haven't seen her sobbing from being harassed and laughed at in school. You weren't there when, as a third grader, she devised a way to get others to stop making fun of her: She announced to everyone that we were moving to Alabama. (Imagine my surprise when the gossip traveled back to me from friends about our sudden plan to move!) You weren't there when a kindergarten classmate told her, "Please shut up! You're giving me a headache!" or at the bus stop when another girl said, in front of the other kids, "We get twenty spelling words every week. How many do YOU get?" (Pointing out that a special ed student gets a reduced workload.) You haven't heard her question "Why can't I be normal?" "Why was I born like this?" "What did I do to deserve this?" You haven't heard her when she says she wishes she were dead.

You haven't been with me in the dark of a sleepless night with a whirling mind questioning fate, God, the universe. Obsessing about how could it happen that my well-planned life, my good fortune at having an education, good health, friends, a devoted, hardworking spouse, a good career, financial security, and all kinds of blessings got out of control to where nothing makes sense and nothing I do to save my child seems to work.

Mental health professionals need to be mindful that we and our child are unique as snowflakes and sometimes just as fragile. My child is not like your child, or any other child. She is not just a "case." Our family is not like your family, or any other family. Above all, we love our damaged children. We need help. Please treat us right.

Professional Help Comes in Two Sizes: Great and Not-So-Helping

"I love my job when I'm not there."

—PAUL R. LINDE, *Danger to Self: On the Front Line with an ER Psychiatrist*

The Not-So-Helping Professionals—I hope no parent ever encounters these, but like all professions, some are better than others. Among our not-great experiences:

» When my son was ten, he reported offhandedly one day that the counseling therapist he had been seeing would often fall asleep during their sessions.

» Our pediatrician referred my son to a highly regarded new psychiatrist and we set up the first appointment. Brendan ran away that day. Knowing I would have to pay for the appointment anyway, I went alone. Perhaps that didn't sit well with the doctor, because as I sat on his couch and sobbed and blubbered my story, he sat coldly, offering no solace. I badly needed a Kleenex. I could have used a whole box. He shrugged. Incredibly, he didn't have any. We never went back to him.

» My daughter's pediatrician referred us to a pediatric neurologist. He spent all of five minutes with us. Without looking me or my four-year-old in the eye, he said, "Typical case of ADHD" and wrote a prescription for Ritalin. The Ritalin turned her into a zombie. We didn't go back.

» When she was nineteen, I took Katherine to see a new psychiatrist. This time I was more conscious of the cost, so I found her in our insurance network. The doctor took a hefty deposit to kick off treatment, then said (in front of my daughter), "Of course, borderline isn't treatable." When we tried to make a subsequent appointment, her assistant said the doctor felt the case was too complicated and that we should find someone else. We were not refunded the deposit.

The Good Guys—We have also encountered dedicated, hard-working, and caring professionals, even if they were confounded and had no easy answers to our situation.

» One of Katherine's many therapists was a young woman who quickly established a bond with my daughter, then in middle school. She was the first who insisted that we attend family therapy as well. No one had ever proposed that before. It helped in more ways than one. Years after Katherine had moved on to a new therapist, this therapist contacted me to ask how Katherine was doing. I would believe it if I were told that even many years later, she still thinks about my daughter.

» Among the many great things that Katherine's long-term therapist, David Mason, did was to visit her when she was hospitalized, offer to attend meetings at her school, come up with alternative ideas for therapeutic approaches, counsel her brothers and her parents about Katherine and other issues, and take many phone calls from her or her parents at night and on weekends. He did not take insurance, but he only raised his rates slightly, and only once. Though he moved away and she doesn't see him regularly any longer, she knows she can call him any time.

» A self-described schizophrenic reports in an online blog that a caring therapist is the reason he is functioning well. He wants others to know that his case is not an easy one:

"I have ADD, ODD, Asperger's (a form of autism), ADHD, and am slight bipolar. I'm not dangerous or a harm to any other person. . . . I'm not something to be feared or rejected. I'm just different. There are worse cases then I, I can tell you that. Some kids can't control themselves and what happens, and yes. Some kids are a danger to themselves and others. But we're not for society to look down upon, or think we're some kinda messed up freak. We need to be understood, we need more people to help us. Some people won't step up to the plate because they're afraid. If more people understood then I think more people would be caring enough to help" (LOHDBR).

Great Help, Great Challenge

Great help can make all the difference in the world. What constitutes great help and what should you look for? Parents of mentally ill children need to know they and their kids are in good, competent, steady, hands. They naturally approach mental health professionals seeking expertise. Often, they expect miracles.

The reality is, working with the mentally ill of any age is very complicated. It can be one of the most difficult lines of work imaginable, so it is important for parents to be knowledgeable about those who would care for their children and to understand the challenges that treatment professionals face.

Their Point of View

Professionals in the behavioral health fields are trained (and therefore expected) to quickly assess and make treatment recommendations for a wide range of difficulties:

» Is a withdrawn child with temper tantrums within the range of normal or is she on the autism spectrum?

» Does a seemingly normal middle schooler who has cried for a week need medication, or will this pass on its own?

» Can the defenses of a belligerent teen who is failing in school be peeled away to reveal if this is just typical adolescent rebellion or something more serious?

» How severe is the depression of a college student who is partying too much and can't get out of bed to go to class? Could this be addiction?

Information from clients and their parents can be unreliable at best. Mentally sick people often are unable to acknowledge their illness, or have a tendency to be dishonest about behavior and symptoms. Professionals must have the intuition and training to separate drug abuse from addiction from illness, and stress from trauma or abuse. Treatment? What kind? Medications? Which one or what combinations? Who will monitor progress—the counselor or the doctor? Will insurance help them pay for it?

It goes without saying that, as in all professions, not all therapists graduated at the top of their class. Theirs is not an exact science; no amount of training or practical experience can guarantee a perfect diagnosis and treatment recommendation without a certain amount of trial and error. They are not gods. They are not magicians. They are human and can make mistakes.

* * *

In her book *Brain on Fire*, Susannah Cahalan shares her story of "my month of madness." Susannah, a healthy young woman, began having strange psychological and physical symptoms that progressed to hospitalization. A psychiatrist diagnosed her as acutely schizophrenic and suffering from alcohol withdrawal, and treated her accordingly. However, when she got worse, further tests and the lucky hunch of another doctor led to the diagnosis of a more threatening, yet treatable, illness of the brain. She was suffering not from madness but rather a rare and potentially lethal viral illness called autoimmune encephalitis. Had the psychiatric diagnosis stood unchallenged, she might not have survived.

* * *

To make things even more complicated, studies have been done and much has been written about burnout in the mental health profession. Understaffing and pay issues contribute to this, but burnout often comes from the personal experience of working in a field where one is required to be devoted to others and set one's own needs aside. It is an unnatural relationship. Patients may never improve. If they do, the counselor may never get the credit, but if they don't, the counselor may get the blame. In the revolving door of patients coming and going, professionals who try to help may never know the outcome. How many of us could work in a profession where we are unsure of how successful we are? No wonder the stress can become intolerable.

I have great sympathy for those in the professions. They must navigate a mental health care system that has been broken for decades and getting worse. No wonder the number of treating professionals to mentally sick people is dwindling. They are caring individuals, or they would not have entered the field. However, because mental illness is not an exact science and is often treatable but generally not curable, quite possibly they suffer a career-long sense of frustration. Cases become intractable. Insurance companies obstruct. Parents are in denial about their child's diagnosis, or they accept it and demand results to sustain their shreds of hope. Patients don't cooperate with recommendations for therapies and medications. Complaints arise about lack of progress. Payment is erratic. Patients die.

Working in this field can be far more challenging than most people in the general public know. Psychiatrist Paul Linde notes that the stigma connected with the mentally ill also affects "… the people associated with it—those crazy psychiatrists." Sometimes, severely ill patients attack. According to an American Psychiatric Association study, "40% of psychiatrists are assaulted during their careers." Physical attacks on mental health professionals who treat the mentally ill in prisons are commonplace. In rare cases, there have been treatment professionals murdered in their offices by patients. Given the attention to violent outbursts and gun slaughter that has occurred in recent years, there is the expectation that treatment professionals should be able to predict—and prevent—violence, even though a wealth of research has shown that in reality, they cannot reliably do this.

Offering further confusion and pressure on mental health practitioners, some recent research offers hope for just the opposite. On the website www.askforhelp.org, Dr. Gerald F. Ronning, MD, a psychiatrist and neurologist in Minneapolis, Minnesota, discusses his research that shows there may actually be ways to predict violence in young people. His view is that the belief that there is no way to prevent tragedies such as Sandy Hook actually leads to "pessimism and failed treatments." His research shows that by interpreting the language of troubled young persons, violent tendencies can be identified, allowing intervention by "applying appropriate, focused measures." Clearly, this is an area where more research is needed to see if this approach can become successful in practice.

* * *

> *"I do not have a psychiatrist and I do not want one, for the simple reason that if he listened to me long enough, he might become disturbed."*

> —JAMES THURBER

Paul Linde offers that, given what mental health workers face on the job, it should come as no surprise that the "occupational hazards for the modern-day psychiatrist include anxiety, depression, alcoholism, addiction, and emotional withdrawal."

If a mental health professional is not frustrated, perhaps she is unnaturally strong—and what does that mean for her work? Is empathy waning? Has acceptance of the difficulties associated with her life's work made her cynical about the outcomes? Maybe she has reached burnout and doesn't even know it. Burnout for mental health workers has been described "as a slow degradation of a counselor's ability to empathize with clients over time" (Shallcross, 2011).

This is not good news. I share it because parents need to understand that professionals you encounter may be dealing with some daunting personal challenges. The counselor you choose may not be a good fit for you, your child, or your family. But keep looking. Your family's future is at stake. Stand your ground on behalf of your child. Know that it is possible to find and come to depend on a good treatment professional, or even better, on a competent, caring team.

Money: Getting What You Pay For

The relationship between patient and provider is further complicated by the fact that money is involved. There is a certain amount of awkwardness in attaching a financial transaction to a one-way relationship of intimacy and trust. Further, it often amounts to sizable amounts of money clients must pay to trust a stranger with the most private problems that lie behind their front door, or behind their eyes. Counselors are trained to deliver a service in a detached, dispassionate, formal, not self-revealing, interactive way. A client may appreciate and understand this approach, may even thrive in being able to share information they can't anywhere else, yet handing over payment may still darkly color the relationship. And those jaded professionals for whom it has become "just a job" are taking money without returning the caring that should underlie the counseling relationship.

Just as there are people who are not suited to be cops or teachers or any other profession, there are some who should not be involved with mental illness. If working with mentally ill children has become just a paycheck, mental health professionals should consider using their training in some other way, or even leaving the field altogether, because treating an emotionally fragile and vulnerable human being and a beaten down, hopeless, and financially stretched family—and doing it well—requires a daunting set of exceptional skills:

» Counseling training
» Broad knowledge of the field
» Ongoing professional development
» Practice and experience
» Ability to set boundaries
» Determination, commitment, and perseverance
» A nurturing heart
» Empathy
» A strong sense of humor
» Resilience in the presence of failure
» Ability to take care of oneself to remain mentally and physically healthy

It isn't always true that "you get what you pay for." There are talented and skilled professionals who charge high fees; there are some who don't. I have seen my daughter receive excellent therapy from a free counselor. When it comes to finding good help, money is and should be a consideration. However, where do you start if you don't have insurance or the financial wherewithal to start? There is help in this area, and you shouldn't feel like you are on your own.

Unfortunately, the availability of help varies by geography, and the right information may be difficult to track down. Some communities offer free or reduced cost mental health services from local government agencies as well as some private organizations. Bear in mind that there is no guarantee that social agencies can provide exactly what your family needs. In addition, there can be problems with availability for services that are in high demand and not sufficiently funded and staffed. The National Alliance on Mental Illness (www.nami.org) and Mental Health America (www.mentalhealthamerica.net) have nationwide affiliates that can point you in the right direction, providing information about what is available in your area.

Share the Care: Teamwork

How can parents and professionals ensure that mentally ill children get the best care possible? My view is that a team approach is one important solution to the problems facing both patients and professionals. By "team" I am not talking about a loosely associated and diverse group of professionals who share rental space. Teamwork to treat an emotionally ill child should be a group of people who all know the child and the family, and who meet and share information regularly and frequently. If all work from the same handbook in a collaborative model, communicating often, the approach to a case would be simplified and focused, and the chances of successful treatment outcomes might be higher.

Who should be on the team? Everyone involved with the child's life and issues:

» Parents and families
» Professionals: psychiatrists, counseling therapists, social workers
» Teachers and tutors
» Special education teachers
» School counselors
» Social skills training programs
» Occupational therapists, speech therapists
» Pediatricians and other medical specialists
» A case manager, if available, to help coordinate services

Any psychiatrist will tell you that it is difficult to get a group of them to agree on how to handle any situation, yet collaboration and collegiality among treating professionals has to be a stronger approach that the haphazard ones that dominate now. Two (or three or four) heads are better than one. Counselors could benefit by broadening their knowledge and perspective. For example, if a therapist makes the determination that a client needs residential treatment, someone on his team should have firsthand knowledge of where to go and would help get the person admitted quickly and efficiently. A team approach would also ensure that no matter what problem arises or when, there is professional backup—someone available to handle the late-night phone call or the weekend meltdown.

This is not unprecedented: obstetricians have always worked this way. When a baby is coming, the obstetrician or a backup physician is immediately available. Like birth, an emotional crisis can happen any time of the day or night, and attention cannot wait. Families and clients need to know they can get help immediately at any time from a familiar professional who is fully informed about their case.

To drive home my point: The disorganized and haphazard way that the situation with Gus Deeds was handled by an array of disconnected mental health professionals led directly to tragedy—a father deeply scarred in face and heart, and a dead son. Another recent case in Virginia involved the Fee family, whose son became psychotic and committed suicide after being treated by several providers who were prescribing an array of medications improperly without consulting or communicating about it.

A side benefit of the team approach is that collaboration can be one way to decrease the stress and promote wellness for individual practitioners. "When counselors are isolated, whether working in rural areas or working as sole private practitioners, maintaining wellness can pose an even bigger challenge. Without other colleagues to learn from, vent with or lean on for support, stress is more likely to build unimpeded. Experts say finding a support system, whether through formal supervision or an informal network of other professionals to meet with for consultation and camaraderie, is vital" (Shallcross, 2011).

In addition, advances in technology should be included in this integrated model to facilitate teamwork. For example, if all on the team have access to the same source of compiled electronic health records, then all information about treatments and medications can be shared and coordinated. This would seem a no-brainer, but it has yet to happen in the widespread, comprehensive way that is needed.

In the current environment, parents must reinvent the wheel over and over in looking for help for their child, each time starting from step one recounting histories, filling out mounds of paperwork about counseling approaches and medications. They are left on their own to be the prime contractor at the top of the pyramid of people involved with their child.

Since the age of three, my daughter has met with many specialists. She has taken dozens of different medications and combinations. I have been managing her case on my own, while there may have been programs and services that could have made it easier had I ever heard of them from any of the experts we consulted. Recently, I attended a meeting of parents of mentally ill children with county officials who preside over mental health issues, and one of the first questions the county representative wanted to know was: "Have you been able to get a bed in county residential treatment when the need arose?" My jaw dropped; I must have looked like a fish pulled from the ocean. "There is residential treatment? In the county? Beds? What beds?"

The system is broken. It is exhausting. It is failing. It has to change. An interconnected team approach would seem a win-win plan for all.

Until Then . . . What?

In lieu of a perfect and future solution, what can parents and professionals do *right now*? Here are a few suggestions:

For Parents

» Speak up. Always be polite and treat professionals with respect, but don't be intimidated or defer your role and responsibility as your child's advocate.

» If some urgent new information or crisis arises, get the information to them, but don't send four-page emails or call every time your child has a hiccup.

» Provide the primary treating professional with contact information and signed releases for all who work with your child. Ask them to consult on a regular basis.

» Facilitate where you can, by asking questions and requesting specific action. Examples:

  - "Help us understand why you are prescribing this new medication/dose."

  - "We agree. My child should be hospitalized. Can you help by contacting them, making the referral, and asking if they can do an intake immediately?"

  - "Will you help me with my insurance company? Here is the person you can talk to at this number."

  - "It would be so helpful if you could attend my child's IEP (Individual Education Plan) meeting at school."

- "We are in the ER after a suicide attempt. The treating doctor here wishes to speak with you."

» Keep a spiral notebook handy and take notes. Don't rely on your memory or your child's or the therapist's memory about anything.

» Show appreciation. Often. Every professional is human being. She may be thinking about your child at three in the morning, just as you are.

For Treating Professionals:

» Share the burden of a case:

- Consult and info-share with other experts, such as teachers and other psychologists.

- Designate a backup professional for when you are not available.

- Set up (and make mandatory) regular family therapy meetings. Give each member a specific simple assignment so they can play a role in treatment.

» At the outset, provide parents a simple, one-page fact sheet about your policies, fees and insurance, availability for phone, email, emergency contacts, school meetings, consultations with other professionals, etc.

» Consider taking insurance. If not, meet the family halfway and keep fees at a level close to what their insurance calls "usual and customary."

» Be flexible about missed appointments. Treat it as a reschedule. The policy of charging for last-minute cancellations (not covered by insurance) is painful and unfair to parents who may be failing in a last minute fight to get a resistant child to an appointment.

» Consider working weekends and take two weekdays off instead.

» Never run out of Kleenex.

You Can Do This

Parenthood is a challenge under the best of circumstances. Even children without special needs must rely on parents to love them and protect them to ensure they eat the right foods, get plenty of fresh air and physical activity, become educated, learn manners and other social behaviors, and get the right medical attention when they are hurt or sick.

When we realize our child needs professional treatment for behavioral and emotional illness, the earlier we take action, the better. Just as we take our baby to the pediatrician for regular "well baby" checkups, we should be mindful as our child grows to watch for healthy behaviors, and when something seems awry, consult a professional. The majority of people you will consult have your best interest and your child's future wellness as a goal, and will work with you to reach it.

CHAPTER TEN

Costs: Financial and Emotional

"The inexorable truth is this:
They might be glad to have me around, but I was
the alpha and the omega of my parents' suffering."

JOHN GREEN, *The Fault in Our Stars*

*I*n the fall of 2013 I got a call to interview for a new teaching job at an amazing school. I felt from the moment I saw the building that this was meant to be. The interview went very well, and I left feeling confident that this was a great fit for me and that I would be offered the job. Within hours, I was thrilled to get the offer. The perfect job for me was in my hands.

I paused. I didn't accept immediately. Suddenly, panic choked me. Could I do this? My optimism and determination began to fizzle as I considered the circumstances at that time: Katherine, pregnant for the second time, was about to deliver by C-section the child of a former boyfriend, a soon-to-be jailed drug dealer. She was emotionally stable for the moment, but we feared the crazy would be unleashed again after the birth. She still had only limited access to her first baby under legal restrictions that required parental supervision (mostly me). Her soon-to-be-ex husband had custody of the baby, but still had no real job or child care other than his parents and us. We had upcoming court dates about divorce, custody, and visitation. We expected further court involvement in the custody of the new baby as well, and the potential of a court fight over the possibility that we would try to force Katherine to give the new baby up for adoption, which seemed the obvious best path at that time.

My gut ached. Realistically, no matter how much I wanted it and was determined to make things work, I couldn't commit myself to a new full-time job under the possibility of my life exploding into chaos just a few weeks into the school year. I would be split like a wishbone between work and home. It would be humiliating to admit to colleagues that I couldn't hack the job, that I couldn't manage family problems. I called the school, turned down my dream job, drank a glass of wine, and cried the rest of the day.

* * *

Having a child with a disability takes its toll on the heart and also on the bank account. The National Institutes of Mental Health (NIMH) found that in 2006, the average expenditures per child for mental health treatment was $1,931, higher than that for adults. The stress of worrying about your child and whether you can afford to get him help is daunting; when education programs, psychotherapy, medications and consultations with other specialists have been tried and seem to have failed, the stress is unbearable. Crisis after crisis brings terror of losing your child, or losing anything left in your financial nest egg. Recent studies have shown that parents of troubled and disabled children suffer so much long-term stress that it actually affects the DNA in their cells and can lead to early aging. There is some truth to the idea of blaming one's children for every gray hair.

There are three main challenges parents of mentally ill children must handle that may drain finances: finding the right school, the right insurance, and the right intervention.

The Right School

When a child has an emotional illness, education becomes important to his mental health as well. This is the world he will inhabit every weekday for many years. The search for the right education program can be as difficult as searching for the proper therapies and proper medications.

Programs may be available in local public school systems for what are termed "emotional disabilities" or "learning disabilities," but often they cannot meet every child's needs, or a child may be denied services because he is deemed unqualified for them. This forces parents to look into private programs, with critical admissions processes and pricey tuitions. Some public school systems will pay for the tuition for a student to attend a private program if it can be proved that the private school provides something the public school cannot. Is such funding easy to get? It depends on the school system, but often it can be a long process of jumping through hoops only to be declined, making appeals, hiring lawyers, and wasting precious time as a child in need suffers academically and emotionally in his current school. If the child needs immediate placement in a new school and it can't wait, parents have to dig into savings or take a loan, anything to scrape together the funds. To add further stress—and this is important to note and accept—there is no guarantee that the move will prove successful in changing the child's experience in school.

Searching for schools and mental health treatment can become a full-time job. There are parents (usually the mother) who have quit their jobs when the management of the life of a disabled child becomes so all-consuming there is nothing left for a job outside the home. Then the financial ability to pay for therapies, medications, and education programs becomes even more difficult.

In the end, all this effort can often prove to be unhelpful to a child's mental health and often makes no difference in her progress. Every situation and every child is unique, and the availability of programs varies from school district to school district. In general, and based on my own experience, I would advise parents to try not to agonize over this and move their child in and out of different schools. It is hard to think about this, but the reality is there may be no perfect school placement for your child. Depending on his age and grade, and the severity of her illness or learning disability, it may be better to stick with the best program available at your neighborhood public school, and supplement at home with tutors, mentors, and counselors. A side benefit of this path is your child can make and keep friends who live nearby, and this often becomes more important to them than schooling.

I raised my children in the Washington, D.C., suburbs, with some of the top public and private schools in the nation. Even with many good options, I made the mistake of changing schools but never found the "perfect" schooling option for my troubled children. Directly related to her disabilities, we moved Katherine to new schools eight times, including to a boarding school a distance from home. Eventually we had to accept that the schools weren't to blame, nor could they be the solution; a troubled child takes her problems with her from school to school.

At times I thought about homeschooling my daughter, but counseling professionals discouraged me from this because they believed that learning to interact with peers and navigate the world away from her mother was an important skill my daughter needed. In retrospect, perhaps we should have tried homeschooling anyway, as her relationships with peers never improved and her education suffered enormously because of her social difficulties.

The Right Insurance

Insurance must have been invented by a sadist.

To give you an example: During her mid-teens, Katherine spent twenty months in a therapeutic wilderness program recommended by her therapist. It seemed the right placement for her at that time, and she was willing to enroll. It cost $4,500 a month, which we had to put on credit cards with the hope of reimbursement from our insurance. The insurance company gave us mixed messages about whether our plan would reimburse us for some or any of this cost. The promise or denial of payment depended on whom you got on the phone on any particular day. And there were many phone calls. This went on regularly during the time she was in the program, and even for many months after she finished the program, as I tried to recoup some of what we had spent. They toyed with us for three years, until they suddenly stopped taking my calls. We never received a penny.

If you have insurance that covers minimal or even extensive mental health treatment, you will most likely still have to dive into your pockets and savings to cover deductibles and copays to get the coverage your child needs. You may spend a lot of time managing a never-ending conflict between coverage, non-coverage, in-network vs. out-of, limits on coverage, fighting the definition of "usual and customary" levels of cost for services, slow reception of reimbursements or decisions on coverage, paperwork, long phone calls, or waits for mail or email. You may spend a long time on hold, only to speak with a low-level insurance clerk who knows nothing about mental health, professional credentials, various approaches to treatment, medications, or anything else that your on-the-job training has given you expertise. It's frustrating and infuriating.

My hope is that even with the glacial pace of change in the health insurance world since the Affordable Care Act and other legislation requiring mental health treatment parity with medical treatment, things will improve. The new law mandates that insurance plans in the exchange marketplace cover mental health and substance abuse services equally as an "essential health benefit." However, if you have a private plan through your employer or Medicaid through your state, the same rules may not apply. For questions or more information, go to www. healthcare.gov/do-marketplace-insurance-plans-cover-mental-health-and-substance-abuse-services/.

With improvements in insurance, I am hopeful that no parent will fear being told "your child is improving so you don't need more treatment coverage" or "your child is not improving so we will end benefits on (date)." Say what? Such experiences are enough to make a parent mentally ill as well.

At times I have cried in frustration as my efforts to help my family encountered so many obstacles every step of the way. How can you get the help you need when:

» Inpatient programs can cost more than a house.

» Programs that are in your insurance company network don't meet your child's needs.

» Your insurance agrees to cover inpatient for a few days, when your child needs weeks or months.

» Treatment facilities have no bed for your child.

In our case, we consulted numerous professionals, none of whom were in our insurance network, or any network, for that matter. Why didn't we find and use the services of in-network professionals listed in our insurance directory? We found professionals by word of mouth, and we trusted each expert we consulted when they referred us to colleagues, or we went to professionals who were recommended by a friend, a pediatrician, or an Internet search who looked like what we needed. On the few occasions we consulted in-network professionals, we found for an assortment of reasons that we were not satisfied with the experience.

Most therapists and therapeutic programs don't want to deal with insurance hassles, and I don't blame them. They would prefer that we, the clients, deal with the paperwork burden, the slow pace of payments, the assessments to "prove" the services are needed. In my experience, we had to fight for every penny in reimbursements and other benefits, and still we bore most of the costs. Between 2000 and 2010 we sank over $250,000 into various mental health programs and treatments, most of which resulted in only short-lived improvements. For that much money, the least we could have expected was a cure. Oh, and a beach house on Barbados.

My recommendation to parents just starting on this journey is the path of least resistance: Do try insurance network professionals first. If it isn't a good match, find another, but the best way to save money is to stay in-network. The recommendations from others may inspire confidence and lower your anxiety, but they may be no better than the ones your insurance company endorses. I have experienced counseling as low as $8 a session (in network), and up to $400 a session (for an out-of-network psychiatrist, requiring filing for partial reimbursement), and both were of equal value. Another point: Changing therapists with the weather will not help your child's progress. Depending on the circumstances, if a therapist you feel is a good match wants to move you onto a new therapist, respectfully negotiate for the relationship to continue. It may seem that consistency doesn't matter to your child, but ultimately it can be an avenue for working on a child's ability to sustain relationships over time, a common problem area for such children.

The Right Intervention

Before they got the call from one of his friends that their twenty-three-year-old son Tommy was using heroin, Mike and Frances thought their son was on the road to a great, normal life. After many years of therapists and medications and schools and counseling, he was working part-time, taking college classes, and he had a lovely, long-term girlfriend.

His life quickly spiraled downward after that relationship ended.

Mike and Frances had to save their son. This wasn't high school pot smoking. This was death in a needle. Tommy's psychiatrist recommended an interventionist, a person who made a career of staging interventions for substance abusers and getting them into a rehab program with the Caron Foundation, which has a network of programs in various parts of the country. The interventionist was retained for $5,000 plus expenses and worked long distance with several of Tommy's friends to help get him into the program. This month-long rehab would be his sixth. Each program cost many thousands of dollars, some of which was covered by insurance, but much of which came from his parents. When Tommy was finally forced into Caron, he stayed only two weeks and then walked away. After several months on the street, during which his parents heard nothing from him, he signed himself into a program in another state. Miraculously, within a few months he chose sobriety and headed down a healthy path. Mike and Frances had no regrets. They were fortunate to be able to scrape together the money from savings and education accounts and it paid off. $50,000 to save their son? Priceless. And yet, outrageous!

* * *

My daughter was fifteen and six weeks into the school year when she was asked to leave a girls boarding school because of her emotional issues. She agreed she needed help and volunteered to go to the residential wilderness program that I previously mentioned. Her long-term therapist was familiar with the program, having worked there in the past. It was an all-girls therapeutic program in the middle of nowhere in southern Virginia. The day we left her there she looked small and scared, yet kept up a smile as she began what would be a long, difficult journey.

As fall became winter, many nights I would awaken, hearing the icy wind outside the window and wonder how she was holding up, sleeping outdoors in a tent in the woods. She was a skinny, nerdy, indoor girl, not sporty or fit. I was sure the outdoors would either fundamentally change her or kill her. Over the months, in fits and starts, she surprised us by becoming a star pupil and accomplishing some things she never would have been able to even think about, including learning to chop wood and dig a privy. She built a wood jockey for firewood and rebuilt hiking trails. She even overcame her fear of bike riding (that went back to that earlier bicycle accident) when she went on a sixty-mile bicycle and hiking trip on the Appalachian Trail. When she graduated from this program, she and we were so proud of all she had been able to accomplish. She was fit, tan, and confident.

But it didn't last. She was home only two months from the woods when her behaviors became worse than when she went away. It was as though she were a rubber band that had been held stretched tight for all that time and was suddenly free to snap. Finally, we had to face the realization that the true measure of her mental illness was now clear only after a decade of various therapies. She would not be cured.

Was the wilderness the right intervention for her? Did we do the right thing? From our perspective, the answer is yes. For the time she was there, she was healthy and safe. She was given time in nature to grow and learn new skills. She developed confidence she had never experienced before. When she left there, she was almost two years older. Two years closer to what we still hoped would be maturity someday. Was it a failure? A waste of money? I don't think so.

CHAPTER ELEVEN

Perseverance and Creativity:
More Important than Money

At one point, we had one kid in college, another in a private high school, and were bearing the enormous rehab and treatment costs for our troubled son and daughter. It was a money hemorrhage that seemed would never end. When the Great Recession hit in 2008, our house and our retirement investments lost a third or more of their value. Budget cutbacks led to me being laid off from my teaching job. Up until that time, we had been more fortunate than most people. For the first time ever, we were scared about our financial stability and our future.

No parent would be surprised to know that even in dire financial situations, taking care of our kids continues to be a priority. However, I learned that money isn't enough. Acting out of desperation led to decisions that were not useful or helpful. It was during this crisis that it became clear that mental illness and addictions are lifelong conditions that must be managed and treated, but cannot be cured. This is where perseverance and creativity of approach become more important than money. With a more realistic focus, the choices must be realistic; little successes celebrated.

* * *

If you are the parent of a child with emotional issues and don't know where to start, or have already tried some approaches that didn't work out, what should you do? Even when it seems nothing can be done, you can't do nothing. This is your child. Your future. You don't have to give up, and there are ways to minimize the emotional and financial costs of facing this challenge.

Here are some suggestions from my own experience.

Do's and Don'ts for Parents:

Do find a way to fund treatment. Any therapy is better than none. Look into what treatments are available in your community on a sliding scale through mental health organizations. If you have insurance, use the network. If you are informed, and lucky, you will find the right therapist, the right meds, and/or the right inpatient program if it is necessary. Do as much as you can before your child reaches the age of eighteen, when your child is within his rights to refuse treatment and your parental influence becomes limited.

Do learn the best way to communicate with your child. According to a recent article on psychcentral.com, poor communication can cause more problems. Avoid statements like "Get busy, and distract yourself." "Don't you want to get better?" "You can snap out of it. Everyone feels this way sometimes." "Pray about it." "Change your attitude and stop focusing on the bad stuff." Instead of giving advice, try to convey concern, support, and willingness to just listen.

Don't rely on "tough love" to help your emotionally ill teenager or young adult. While the time may come when you feel you must kick your child out of the house, understand that it will not "teach him a lesson," or make her "snap out of it." If your child runs away and chooses to live on the street, it may very well make him worse. Kids on their own will develop streetwise skills. They will shoplift and panhandle. They will associate with criminals and other twisted souls on the street, a training ground for more dysfunction. Girls, in particular, are vulnerable to rape and being drawn into prostitution. Keeping her in your family and in treatment should be the goal and a condition of her staying or returning to your home. But don't let it become a revolving door.

Don't let your over-eighteen child return to stay in your home after he has been on the street. Homelessness is not a method of mental health treatment. When he decides he wants to come home, it is not because he has changed; it is because he is hungry, tired, dirty, and has run out of friends to mooch off.

Allowing him back into your home will disrupt the peace you are enjoying at home without him there, and it will enable him to get back on his feet so he can resume his destructive behaviors. Again, make being in treatment a condition of him spending even a brief time your home.

Don't expect a twenty-eight-day program to cure anything. The best an intensive, short-term program can do is help a substance abuser safely through the physical hell of detox, and then teach her the skills to help her stay sober. Be aware that after discharge, rehab programs often recommend an addict transition to a "sober living community." Sounds well and good, but putting addicts all together in one place is like crowding an elevator with flu patients. Relapse is common, and contagious. There is a reason why the word "rehab" has become something of a joke. Stories about repeated visits to rehab abound, and some research has indicated that the twenty-eight-day programs do not follow a medical model so much as a business (i.e., moneymaking) model. Ultimately, addiction, as well as mental illness, must be managed long-term by the individual, and can only come about when she herself decides to live a different life using the skills recommended in the treatment program. Again, don't let rehab become a revolving door.

Do consider a wilderness program; it will change (not cure) your kid. It is mentally and physically healthy to spend time in the outdoors, endure physical challenges, and commune with and appreciate the beauty of nature. Some cool camping and survival skills will come from it, and your child will become physically strong and fit. He will learn ways to navigate relationships and take responsibility for his behavior and its consequences. Great, as far as it goes, but don't expect too much. The learned skills can quickly disappear when your child returns to daily living and finds them inapplicable. Nevertheless, it can be a valuable growing experience. Years after, he may say it helped.

Do take care of your own needs and wellness. Enrolling your child in a program away from home for a length of time is worth every penny in some major ways. Whether it is boarding school, summer camp, or a residential mental health program, the major benefit is that you will have respite. You will enjoy renewed hope that the experience will help your child. You can sleep knowing your child is safe and someone else's responsibility for a time. Now you can devote your energies and emotions to taking care of your own and your family's needs that have been on the back burner: your health and wellness, maintaining friendships, reinvesting in your relationships with your spouse and other children.

Unless finances are unlimited, don't send your child away to more than one program. Long-term programs offer similar experiences, and repeating is not necessarily helpful. Unless you need to send your child away from home for his or anyone else's respite or safety, save your money for ongoing, regular outpatient therapy with the same therapist, assuming your child has a trusting relationship with him/her and can build on the coping skills learned in the residential program.

Do expect relapses. Keep in mind that mental illness and addiction require a lifelong struggle. Depending on the seriousness of the diagnosis, periods of stability may be cyclical.

If your child has been in one long-term program and relapses, some "booster treatment" outpatient therapy or a week of day treatment may be needed, but a succession of long-term programs will probably not make things better.

Don't make it easy. As your child grows older and makes decisions for himself, don't do for him what he can and must do for himself. Enabling makes it possible for him to continue risky behaviors. Help, but don't enable. That means avoiding such things as bailing her out of jail, sending her money, allowing her to live in your basement rent-free. It is one of the hardest things for a parent to do, but give your child the space and dignity to make his own decisions and mistakes. That is the only way she can learn to take care of herself.

Do let go when the time comes. As you grow older, the time will come to wean yourself from the belief that it is your job to affect the daily life and decisions of your children. As they grow older and more independent, they will make choices you may not like. This is a normal step in every parent-child relationship, but tends to come later and with much trepidation when you have an emotionally ill child. In the years of therapeutic interventions, your child will learn how to take care of herself, and then within the parameters of the illness, she can choose to live her healthiest life. Or not. Your adult son or daughter may always depend on you for emotional and/or some financial support, but ultimately they will be on their own. In the meantime, you can make choices as to what you will do if it is helpful to them, and what you will no longer do if it is not.

Do's and Don'ts for Professionals:

Do be as honest as you feel you can be with parents about mental illness. You must walk a fine line between discouraging them and holding out hope for the future. Much depends on the child's age and diagnosis, but help them understand that it is a chronic condition that can be treated. Make sure they understand what medications and therapies you are recommending and why. Get them on the team.

Do familiarize yourself with inpatient and residential programs. Visit them. Talk to the staff. If hospitalization becomes necessary, parents need to rely on your recommendations. Have information and contact information on local placements as well as distant, so that the client is placed in the program most likely to help.

If you are a therapist and are not a medical doctor who can prescribe psychiatric medicines, ***do have a close working relationship with a psychiatrist*** and consult regularly on how your client is doing. If the counselor and the doctor do not talk regularly, both will be in the dark about how their separate treatments are faring together.

Don't give up on a child or the family. The diagnosis may be challenging, but the longer you work with them, the more likely you will see progress and success. If the diagnosis becomes too difficult for your training and experience, make a referral to a new therapist, but know that sending a family from this professional to that one increases the child's self-image that she is damaged, sick, and hopeless.

Success is Possible.

With abundant and broad commitment, perseverance, and love, there can be positive outcomes. Many mentally ill adults—including my children—are able to hold jobs, go to school, sustain relationships, and take care of their psychological and medical needs. They both must be vigilant to care for themselves each and every day, but then, don't we all need to do that?

The only sure thing is that our children will flounder and fail if they don't get help from caring, knowledgeable adults. That's where parents, teachers, doctors, and psychiatric professionals come in.

* * *

"Our greatest weakness lies in giving up.
The most certain way to succeed is always
to try just one more time."

—THOMAS EDISON

CHAPTER TWELVE:

Inpatient Adventures

"People ask, How did you get in there? What they really want to know is if they are likely to end up in there as well. I can't answer the real question. All I can tell them is, It's easy."

—SUSANNA KAYSEN, *Girl, Interrupted*

One of the hardest things in the world to do is get a mentally unstable person into a safe, long-term (inpatient or outpatient) treatment program. Regardless of how old and how sick your child is, or how much you know he needs major, long-term help, it isn't easy. There are obstacles every step of the way, while the situation worsens day by day.

When we learned from one of his friends that Brendan had relapsed in his recovery, we drove 500 miles and showed up at his apartment to intervene and force him into treatment. He was furious and ashamed, and denied he needed help. We told him we would stay and not let him leave his apartment until he agreed to go with us back into treatment. After many tense hours he reluctantly agreed to get in the car and we drove him there, only to be turned away, saying, "We don't do intakes on Sundays." We had missed our opportunity. By Monday he was again uncooperative, telling us to go away and leave him alone. Defeated, we made the long drive home while trying to devise a new plan to save him. We felt hopeless and alone.

As we careened from crisis to crisis with my daughter, I spent hundreds of hours online and on the phone, trying to find any place I could send her where she would be safe and get the treatment she needed. On one occasion, I sat in my parked car in a rainstorm, crying in frustration because Katherine was making suicidal threats. I had called every local hospital to find out if they could take her immediately. I was told to rely on out-patient treatment; I told them she needed more than a Band-Aid. Clearly, she needed what the professionals refer to as a "higher level of care," yet such a level couldn't be found. It had to be a residential program, because she kept running away, going on and off meds and in and out of regular counseling. One nurse I spoke with was sympathetic, but unable to help. "Yeah, we used to have an inpatient program, but not anymore." She could not refer me elsewhere. "Sorry, I don't know what to tell you." I got the same answers from my daughter's regular counselor and treating psychiatrist.

How could healthcare professionals NOT know of a place for my daughter?

Some hospitals told me that suicidal threats weren't enough to get a bed. "We only take people with drug problems." Sometimes I was asked if we have insurance before being asked, "Is she threatening to hurt herself or anyone else?" On another occasion I called the mobile psychiatric unit to ask them to pick her up and take her in for observation. They said they would do their best, but it might be a day or two before they could get to her. They had so many calls . . .

Some places wouldn't even talk to a concerned parent with an adult mentally unstable child: "Wish I could talk to you, but ... HIPAA laws, you know." Even when I told them I had legal guardianship of my daughter, they wanted immediate documentation and still were unsure what that meant for what they could tell me. There were moments when I prayed she would get arrested for something; at least in jail she would have a roof over her head, a bed, and three meals a day. My prayers went unanswered.

* * *

Often, the first problem a parent encounters is convincing the person to agree that they need treatment. There is a symptom of mental illness called *anosagnosia*, which means "impaired or a lack of awareness." Mentally ill persons are often unable to see that they are in trouble and need help. Parents of under-eighteen children have had to resort to hiring "adolescent escorts" (for a hefty fee) who surprise the teen and forcibly take them away to treatment. In my family, we engaged such services *three times*. Imagine the look of shock and fear on your child's face when hulking strangers, intimidating "thugs," show up at your house. Imagine feeling the guilt of having betrayed your child's trust.

If the child is a legal adult (eighteen or over), they cannot be forced into a residential program without consent. Even if a parent seeks and obtains legal guardianship or power of attorney (as we did), there are still serious limitations on what power is conveyed. My daughter went voluntarily to several programs, but resisted others when she was her sickest and needed it most. What an emotionally sick person needs, yet often doesn't understand or accept, is a comprehensive, integrated, holistic program of nutrition, exercise, and sleep, paired with counseling and medication prescription and monitoring—a caring environment where progress is measured and monitored. Just as important is follow-up monitoring and an open door for continuing treatment, as needed. This must happen over a long period of time. This need is rarely met, because it is nearly impossible to find, and if it can be found there are too many obstacles. The erratic lifestyle of a mentally ill person often leads to stops and starts in medications and counseling at different locations, with different people. Time, energy, and money are wasted on these false starts.

Insurance companies don't help. In fact, they hinder. They offer only a limited list of "in-network" treatment programs; they enforce a limit to the number of days the person can avail themselves of any program (usually twenty-eight days or less, which is far less than what is usually needed); they drag out decisions on reimbursements for out-of-pocket expenses for non-network providers.

* * *

In Justin Torres' short story "In the Reign of King Moonracer," the narrator is an inpatient at a mental hospital. He befriends another patient who likens the hospital to the Island of Misfit Toys in the *Rudolph the Red-nosed Reindeer* Christmas story. In that TV movie, the lion who rules the island, King Moonracer, "… brings them toys to the island, protects them from their own damn cowardice. But what he ought to do is teach them how to deal. … Them toys got to decide they can live in this world, loved or unloved. Quit hoping for something better, some Christmas Miracle. It's the hope that hurts."

* * *

So, how helpful are any inpatient programs, anyway? I can share one experience:

"Mom, I'm in Dominion Hospital."

"How did you get *there*?"

"My friends brought me here last night because I was feeling suicidal. Anyway, just please come and get me. I don't like it here."

"It's a mental hospital. Don't expect room service or chocolates on your pillow."

"Mom, please! I need a ride."

"Have they talked with your regular psychiatrist or therapist?"

"I don't know."

Dominion Hospital is the only short-term inpatient mental health facility in the Northern Virginia area (there are no local long-term programs). It seems every family who has experienced a mental health emergency has spent time in their waiting room. Mention Dominion, and there are sighs and eye-rolls. It has a so-so reputation, but then, how "nice" can a mental hospital be? I did know that one of my daughter's former psychiatrists worked there, so for a minute or two I was glad she was there and hoped some kind of intervention was in the works.

She had been on the street for weeks. She was not eating, not taking meds, sleeping here and there with friends or wherever she could find a place. I use the term "friends" loosely here. These people would not be my first choice for her to spend time with: people with whom she had skipped school and smoked cigarettes and pot, who had introduced her to sexual activity, and at times had even hidden her from me when I was combing the neighborhood looking for her. But I had a glimmer of hope: if these people of questionable character had taken her to the hospital, maybe she would finally take her illness seriously.

When she would leave home for days and weeks at a time this way, we had a "tough love" policy: no help from us, financial or otherwise, unless she agreed to go to an inpatient program to get stabilized physically and emotionally and back on meds. At this point she was over eighteen, and our position was the only leverage we had to try to force treatment. Regularly, she would exhaust her friendships and return home, agreeing to ramp up and cooperate with her treatments, but always refusing to go into any long-term residential program. She would spend a few days and weeks with us, long enough get cleaned up, catch up on her sleep, get some decent food. Then it wouldn't be long before she would disappear again.

When we learned she was in Dominion we thought we finally had an opportunity to hold her in a safe place with some psychiatric treatment until we could find a long-term residential program somewhere in the country. That is not how it turned out. In the twenty-four hours that she was there, the staff never contacted us, because she was over eighteen, even though she had signed a HIPAA release. They did not contact her psychiatrist or regular therapist. They took her word that her diagnosis was "bipolar," and that she wasn't really suicidal. They took her word that she might be pregnant. They finally did a pregnancy test and it was negative. They allowed her to bum cigarettes and smoke. She flirted with a male patient and made plans to date him when they got out. She told us everyone there thought they were a "cute couple."

We spent several hours at the hospital trying to get someone to help us to keep her there. We never met with any treating professional, never could get a straight story on why she was there and what the doctors there had done (or not done) to treat her. They never consulted with her local psychiatrist or psychotherapist.

She showed up in the lobby, discharged.

Once again, we were left angry, disappointed, and discouraged.

* * *

I like to think I am trainable, but it took a long time for me to realize that we were on a fruitless merry-go-round of treatment efforts and programs, only to have her relapse and need another. She had already been away for six weeks in boarding school, followed by twenty months in the wilderness, then two summers at a nine-week camp in upstate New York designed for teens with learning and emotional issues. Here we were again, looking for a place to send her away. It was incredible to me that neither her local psychiatrist nor her therapist knew of residential programs anywhere they could recommend. Her psychiatrist had tried many different medications and combinations, but Katherine never took them long enough to see if they were working. Her therapist cautioned us about sending her out of state to any program for fear she would run away, be lost in an area unfamiliar to her and to us, and fall prey to even worse people. However, for her safety and long-term stabilization, it seemed she had to be kept in one place long enough to give her medications a good run to see if they could be effective. Trying to pin her down to treatment was like tacking Jell-o to a wall.

My hours of research on the Internet yielded only a few programs that looked like they might work for us. There was the problem of her erratic agreement, then disagreement, about going residential. There was a lack of beds and waiting lists. There were cost and insurance obstacles. The highest rated and most worthwhile ones were way beyond our budget.

For example, the Menninger Clinic, which had relocated from Topeka, Kansas, to Houston, was well known to us because Katherine's brother had spent time in treatment there years before. It has always been highly rated, in the top five in the nation, and offered a program designed for young adults. It appeared to be a perfect fit for what we thought Katherine needed. However, it was no longer in our insurance network. It would have required some $1,500 per day (not a typo: $1,500) for a minimum eight-week stay. $84,000! Really? Who has that kind of money? Oscar winners and rock stars, I guess. Even if I could print money in my basement I would think twice before spending that much on any program, which would then involve a protracted and agonizing process to try to obtain partial reimbursement from our insurance company. Understanding that mental illness is treatable but generally not curable, and in my daughter's case, relapse so common, it seems that charging so much for treatment cruelly preys on the desperation of families (wealthy families, that is).

Each time our wayward daughter returned home from the street, it was with the condition that she get into residential treatment and back on meds. She usually agreed reluctantly that she needed help, and I would return to my Internet searches, sending out emails and making phone calls for a program somewhere, anywhere. At one point I found Fulshear Academy near Houston, for girls eighteen and over who were struggling with emotional and academic issues and substance abuse. It is one of only two or three programs in the United States that offered what she needed: A women-only, long-term therapeutic residential program offering dialectical behavioral therapy (DBT), the recommended course for someone with a borderline diagnosis. Further, Katherine could stabilize and, when ready, step down to an apartment with supervision and attend school or a job, and eventually be independent, with long-term follow-up. It was outside of Houston, where we had relatives who could look in on her from time to time and offer help if needed. Most important, it was something we could scrape together the money to fund. We had to come up with $5,000 a month, and Fulshear promised to help us recoup much of it from our health insurance. Katherine said it sounded good to her, and she wanted to go. We made the application and the admissions officer interviewed her, and us, over the phone. She was accepted, and within a week she and I flew to Houston together. The Academy was out in farm country and had horses for the girls to ride. There was a swimming pool and a new, modern central building with a large new kitchen. The cabins where the girls lived were clean and comfortable. The staff all seemed capable and caring and not at all intimidated by our daughter's complex problems.

When I left her there, I had renewed hope that finally, we had turned a corner. Katherine would be away from the temptation of boys, get the therapy she needed, do some horseback riding, make some friends her own age, and eventually get a job. She would live near caring relatives. It all should have worked so well.

How naïve and delusional I was. Her local therapist's concerns about sending her far from home proved to be correct. She signed herself out of Fulshear after less than a week and took to the streets again. Unable to keep her against her will, they had to let her leave. She spent time living with strangers, time in a mental hospital, and several months living with an ex-heroin addict alcoholic twice her age. When she called us and asked to come home, he imprisoned her at gunpoint. Police were called, and local relatives had to rescue her. They took her to the airport and she returned home, having promised to immediately attend the local partial hospitalization treatment program for at least several weeks until we could find another safe residential program somewhere else.

She was a mess—tired, depressed, emaciated and, we were all stunned to learn several weeks later, HIV positive. That didn't stop her. In fact, it made her run away again, this time to escape and deny this devastating diagnosis.

When she returned several months later, she was very sick. And pregnant.

* * *

Later that year, after she had eloped with a new boyfriend who promised to help her raise her baby and during her experience of postpartum insanity, I tried to get her into the Hill Center for Women at the Mclean Hospital in Boston. It seemed another perfect program that offered what she needed. She was more than willing. Mclean Hospital is well known and for decades has enjoyed an excellent reputation as one of the top inpatient facilities in the country. Katherine agreed she needed inpatient, long-term psychiatric care. We, along with her new husband and his family, agreed to help with her baby while she got well.

The Center kept us hanging for many months. During that time, her mental health deteriorated and she disappeared again, this time with an old boyfriend, leaving her newborn behind. She went to Vermont and then Massachusetts, and for the next several months she lived in and out of New England shelters. At one point, we were able to get her to agree to go into Arbor Fuller (A-F) Hospital in Attleboro, Massachusetts. Her brother Brendan drove three hours in a blizzard to pick her up and take her there. She spent Christmas in the hospital, but after less than two weeks, she left with her boyfriend (who was in violation of his Virginia probation), and they hit the streets again. All this time the staff at A-F was trying to get her stabilized and transferred into the Hill Center, while the Hill Center kept delaying, asking for repeated updated paperwork, giving us encouraging words with every phone call I made to them, yet never accepting her.

Months later, when they finally made a decision not to accept Katherine into their program, they did so without ever meeting her. Worse, they didn't have the integrity to tell us directly. They simply stopped taking our phone calls. They contacted her Virginia therapist to engage him to be the one to tell us. They didn't explain their decision. This, from one of the most prestigious mental health treatment facilities in the country! Their foot-dragging had catastrophic consequences for us: Katherine and her boyfriend lived in shelters in Massachusetts in the dead of winter for several months. And, she became pregnant again.

Sisyphus had it easy. He only had to roll a boulder uphill for eternity.

CHAPTER THIRTEEN

Crisis Intervention by First Responders

*"They said your son is good to go. . . . I told them
he was going to kill himself." A parent whose son
committed suicide shortly after being released
from a psychiatric facility. (CNN.com)*

According to a 2010 ranking published by www.
uslifeexpectancy.com, suicide and homicide are
leading causes of death for Americans ages fifteen through twenty-four, ranking second and fourth out of fifty causes of death.
Most of these are connected in some way to mental illness. The
problem is growing, especially when you consider the number
of cases of post-traumatic stress disorder (PTSD) suffered by
soldiers returning from two wars that have been ongoing for
more than a decade.

Enough has been said about guns, and enough sympathy
has been thrown around like confetti. To paraphrase Richard

Martinez, father of a son shot and killed by Elliott Rodger in the Santa Barbara violence, when a member of Congress called to offer sympathy, "I don't give a shit about your sympathy. Do something!" His grief has become a catalyst for activism, quoting the catchphrase, "NOT ONE MORE!"

What can be done? What efforts are being made already? Where are we going wrong? One area that needs to be addressed is the role played by first responders—police and EMTs, who are highly likely to encounter mentally ill people in the course of their work. A three-city study found that 92 percent of patrol officers had at least one such encounter in the previous month (Borum, et al, at the Bill Booth blog).

* * *

On more than one occasion, the local county crisis intervention unit has been called to visit my daughter and assess her reactive outbursts and suicide threats. In one instance, they were unable to respond immediately due to the number of calls and the limited number of responders they had. By the time they got to her, a day or two later, the crisis had passed. On other occasions, she was able to pull herself together, put on her "calm, pretty, smiling, polite, grateful" demeanor, and send them away. She was able to do the same for the EMTs after an ambulance was called when she had an inexplicable seizure. She refused to go back to the hospital, where the day before she had prematurely discharged herself only thirty-six hours earlier she had major surgery—a C-section to deliver her baby—and she was still on major narcotic pain treatment. But, as it goes in these situations, she could not be forcibly hospitalized by anyone, despite it being the obvious course of action. Within weeks, she had left her husband and baby and disappeared.

* * *

In Purcellville, Virginia, Christian Sierra, a high school junior, age seventeen, became depressed while hanging out with a friend. When he began to cut himself with a knife, the friend called 911. Christian ran away in fear when confronted, still waving the knife. A police officer pulled his service revolver and fired. The boy is dead. He was a student at the local public high school, an athlete who had many friends. His parents say he was depressed but not violent. Fox news reported that, "What continues to gnaw at the family is whether officers could have handled this differently. Was the officer who fired properly trained for someone who is suicidal? Did he have a Taser that could have been used instead? What was the role of the other officers on the scene? The family can't understand how this could have happened."

* * *

A month before Elliott Rodger killed himself after murdering six and injuring a dozen more in Santa Barbara, he was confronted by police who were sent to assess him based on information from his concerned parents. They said he was acting irrationally and talking of suicide. Elliott was able to convince the police that it was just a misunderstanding; that he was okay, not suicidal. The police found him stable and polite and did not check on his ownership of firearms, dismissing his parents' concerns. Elliott's fourteen-page autobiography, seen only after the tragedy, demonstrated how disturbed this young man was and described his ability to seem normal, to fool everyone about his thoughts and intentions. He was quite capable of "hiding under the radar," as the local sheriff put it after the killings.

* * *

Too often, first responders do not have the needed training and temperament to handle these situations to a helpful outcome. Tragically, as we have seen in many recent news stories, especially if it involves an African American who is exhibiting irrational behavior, too often a police officer responds with violence.

First responders have to do better.

How could these situations have had a different outcome? Funding, training, increased personnel, or legislation—we must demand whatever it takes to address these inexplicable and unacceptable occurrences. There are a number of measures that might have made a difference, but with regard to crisis responders called in to help, it is clear they need more time with the individual, more skills to judge the status of his/her emotions and thinking, to be more familiar with the treatment the troubled person may currently be receiving, and to put more credence in those closest to the individual who have asked for help. If increased assessment skills could save even one life, it would be worth funding and implementing changes such as the following:

» Law enforcement professionals and other emergency first responders nationwide must be required to take and pass comprehensive Crisis Intervention Training (CIT). Training in place now must be reviewed and improved so that every crisis unit will be fully prepared to assess and handle a mentally unstable person.

» When they are called to check on a troubled person, they should be accompanied by a psychiatrist so that a more reliable and skilled psychiatric assessment can be made.

» Responders must take more seriously the information and concerns of the parents or friends who have called for help. They must look deeper than the initial demeanor of the person they are assessing, and they must investigate whether the person has dangerous weapons in his possession. It is not uncommon for some mentally ill people to appear "normal" when it serves their purpose, i.e., to avoid arrest or involuntary psychiatric care.

» When police respond to a call about an unstable person, they should be thoughtful about how armed they need to be. In most cases, deadly force is not needed. Additional backup personnel, pepper spray, or Tasers should be sufficient.

» When such an incident occurs, local social services should remain on the case going forward, checking in on a regular basis with the individual and his family so that a troubled person doesn't become either a perpetrator or a victim of crime.

» The bar must be lowered to something more actionable than simply "imminent danger to self or others." Even the most skilled psychiatrists cannot predict violence with total accuracy. Family members who know the person cannot be relied upon to predict imminent violence, either. There are too many cases where after a homicide or suicide, even those closest to the mentally ill person say they had not imagined such a tragedy was coming. The need for a warrant to search the mentally ill person and/or their car or home for weapons can hinder a timely intervention. Legislative remedies may be needed to facilitate actions that may prevent a tragedy.

We're Working on It:

Some changes along these lines are happening.

In 2015, the Gloucester, Massachusetts police department instituted a new program that is catching on across the country in places like Groton, Connecticut; Port Angeles, Washington; and Rolling Meadows, Illinois. The Police Assisted Addiction and Recovery Initiative (**PAARI**) is a nonprofit organization to change the approach to drug offenders from arresting them to getting them help. It is a more humane view of addiction: to see it as a disease rather than a crime, and to facilitate treatment, not incarceration.

Recently, the national organization Treatment Advocacy Center honored **Congressman Tim Murphy** for his advocacy for changes in laws connected with mental health. He is experienced as a psychologist before coming to Washington. He has held hearings and authored legislation. "The 'Helping Families in

Mental Health Crisis Act' includes provisions to increase the use of court-ordered outpatient treatment for qualifying individuals with untreated mental illness and increased psychiatric hospital beds, clarify HIPAA and decrease the criminalization for mental illness, among other important provisions."

Another example: The police force in **Tulsa, Oklahoma,** which experiences some 800–900 calls a month to respond to a mental health emergency, has instituted forty hours of mental health training to all academy personnel so that they can respond thoughtfully and peacefully to these types of crises, and so that the sick person gets health services instead of incarceration. Police are trained to drive the person to wherever there is a bed, which can be as far as 100 miles away.

The **Mental Health First Aid Program** is a public education program sponsored by the National Council of Behavioral Health and the Missouri Department of Mental Health to train people on ways to identify, understand, and respond to a person in a mental health crisis. Some 500,000 people have been trained. It is a national program, but the top five states that have trained the most people are California, Pennsylvania, Texas, Michigan, and Missouri. For more information on bringing this training to your area, go to www.mentalhealthfirstaid.org.

These are baby steps in the right direction. We need more, or the violence will continue. What is needed is bold, nationwide progress.

CHAPTER FOURTEEN

What Parents Must Do to Survive

"Your love is thick and it swallowed me whole."

—ALANIS MORRISSETTE, *Head over Feet*

S urvival means more than getting through the trauma of having a mentally disabled child. It means taking care of yourself and your family, while remaining engaged and concerned about the well-being, survival, and future of that child, who becomes a priority. Helping the special needs child takes an enormous amount of time, energy, and focus. In the process, we often neglect our own needs.

* * *

Donna stopped going regularly to her doctor because her resources were taken up with caring for her emotionally ill daughter. She ignored a lump, until it had metastasized. Donna's physical, emotional, and financial resources were decimated even further over the next year as she endured cancer treatment and her daughter failed to improve.

* * *

Phil and Terry stopped taking vacations and dining out because they both felt guilty for not being there for their son if he needed them—and he usually did—and because they were afraid to leave him in anyone else's care. Over time, their marriage began to suffer. They eventually divorced.

* * *

Maggie had a job she loved in public affairs of a government agency. She and her husband, Jack, shared family duties caring for their two school-age children, including a son, Ben, who had an emotional disorder. When Ben's middle school expelled him for bringing a knife to school, it was the final straw. It led to Maggie quitting her job to devote more time to finding him a new school, monitoring his behaviors, managing his treatments, and keeping up with the needs of his siblings. Not only did this cut the family income, but Maggie's career was cut short, which left her depressed and hopeless.

* * *

Will My Life Ever Be Mine?

Mental illness and fairness are two planets separated by a hundred universes.

After a ten-year break during which I devoted myself to raising my children, I went back to college to become certified as an educator. Soon I returned to full-time work as a teacher in the fall of 2006. The timing seemed optimal. My three sons were grown and gone to college and work and moving on with their lives, and Katherine was away as well, first at a boarding school, then at a therapeutic boarding school. For the next two school years, I was at the top of my game and loving my job.

My third year, Katherine was back home, her emotional turmoil a daily roller coaster. There were increasing numbers of counseling appointments, frantic calls to her psychiatrist and counselor, teacher conferences, screaming fights at home. At the same time, Brendan relapsed and quit college, and my husband's eighty-five-year-old mother fell and broke her hip, requiring my caregiving attention. Soon after, my own mother suffered several health problems and had to be moved out of Florida and closer to family, much against her wishes. Everything came crashing down at the same time.

I had always been someone who could compartmentalize my life, keeping the crazy at home separate from my cool competence at work. One day I burst into tears at school for no apparent reason. My director asked if it was pressures at school or at home and I had to admit it was trouble at home, though

I didn't go into the details. She was very understanding, telling me, "We all have private lives. There are always things we deal with at home. It's okay."

For me, it was not okay. Personal problems began to consume my whole life. I began to suffer attacks of anxiety at school, began to take personally any small problem that came along with a student. I wondered if I needed to take a year off. But I loved my work! I had beautiful, supportive colleagues; my students and their parents seemed to love me; the girls I taught were lovely and smart and healthy. They were not sick, like my daughter. Time off from what I loved would be giving in to the insanity at home. It would be giving up the one area of my life that was sane. It would curtail the plan I had for my life, which was to teach for a decade or more and then retire.

Then, an earthquake hit me when contract signing time came in the spring and I was told that the Great Recession had driven down enrollment; the school had to institute severe budget cuts, forcing layoffs of several teachers. I would not be renewed for the following year. My plan for my future fell off a cliff. Stunned and heartbroken, I went through the following days and months in a fog, not letting on that I was devastated, trying not to cry at school. I had to deal with problems at home and continue at work as if things were okay. I couldn't let my students down.

My confidence tanked. I begin to wonder if my personal problems had bled into my daily work. I would have to slap myself to keep from thinking they let me go for more than budgetary reasons. In the ensuing months, I tried to find another teaching job with no success. My unemployment stretched into years. Depression set in as I questioned my talents and abilities.

Gradually, I coped by acknowledging to myself that accepting a new full-time teaching job would have been impossible while dealing with the nightmare my daughter was wreaking on our family. Eventually, I rebelled. This was not going to consume my life. "If I'm not earning, I'd better be learning." Thoughts of all the obstacles were set aside, as I considered taking care of my own needs for a change. Everyone else would just have to deal. For two years I concentrated on getting a Master's degree in education from the University of Virginia. With an enhanced resume, I was certain I'd be able to return to teaching. My graduate school experience was so fulfilling and successful that it renewed my pride and confidence, and I nearly kissed the diploma when I had it in my hand.

* * *

It is important to remember throughout the experience of raising a child with emotional illness that parents have choices. Let me repeat that: You have CHOICES. That means you can choose to quit your job to parent your child. Or not. You can choose to focus more on your marriage first and your child second. Or not. It is a choice to put a child's health needs ahead of your own. In the long run, it is empowering to know that while fate has dealt you a bad hand, you can play that hand any way you choose. You can take care of yourself and your family while doing your best to meet the needs of your child. In fact, taking care of yourself is one of the ways you will be able to meet those needs.

First Things First

When a climber takes on a mountain, he makes sure he has the appropriate equipment and skills so he can survive and make it to the top. Survival as a parent of a child with challenges is no different; it means learning and using professional skills with your child. As indicated in a previous chapter, many of the skills that make for an exceptional treatment professional must be part of the parents' repertoire as well, not only for survival, but also to be best equipped to meet the challenge of helping your child as much as possible without destroying your own life. The most critical skills include:

- » Ability to set boundaries and stick with them
- » Determination, commitment, and perseverance
- » A nurturing heart
- » Empathy
- » A strong sense of humor
- » Resilience in the presence of failure
- » Acceptance of the limitations inherent in the situation
- » Willingness to ask for help
- » Ability to care for one's own mental and physical health in the face of adversity
- » Health literacy. Learn the jargon of the mental and behavioral health universe.

Some of these skills—the commitment and nurturing heart, for example—probably already came naturally with your child's arrival. If you have perseverance to the point of tenacity, you will defy obstacles and overcome adversity to find ways to acquire the necessary knowledge about your child's needs (and yours). You can learn about how to talk to an unstable person. You can learn what boundaries are and how to set and sustain them. You can learn about the latest developments in medications, treatments, programs, insurance policies, and strategies. You can temper your hopelessness by joining support groups or simply by hanging out more often with trusted friends who help you laugh when you want to cry.

You can keep looking until you find the right doctors and counselors: professionals with the right skills to treat your child who are caring people who won't give up. You can overcome your need to isolate yourself in shame and depression and instead get counseling yourself from a skilled professional.

Taking Care of Yourself

As you are caring for your child, there are things you can do to help and support yourself. Your own well-being is as important as your child's. Beyond the obvious, such as eating healthily and getting enough sleep and regular exercise, the following are some things I have tried that have helped me.

Spirituality can provide strength. Many of us find support by participating in activities that comfort us through spirituality. What you involve yourself in doesn't have to be religious; in fact,

I find organized religion is not as helpful as private meditation. Connecting with a power greater than oneself, outside of oneself, helps you to feel that you are not alone. It helps when despair threatens to destroy you, when you are tempted to ask, "Why, God? Why me?"

Be it meditation, yoga, communing with nature through hiking, biking, camping, gardening, or attending some kind of worship services, any and all of these things can help you cultivate inner peace. Your child can also benefit from learning about his connection to the universe, especially later in life when he is seeking emotional and spiritual strength on his own. Start your children when they are young in these activities and you will know you have laid a foundation of good spirituality, even if the day comes when they seem to have no moral code and profess to believe in nothing.

Work at keeping perspective. It helps me to remain conscious of the fact that as bad as it gets at times, it could be worse. Look around and you will see others who are facing challenges you imagine you couldn't handle. When people who know my situation ask me how I am able to survive, I tell them that I am not exceptional; I'm not the only person on the planet who has had a troubled or special needs child. Many others have faced similar challenges and have surprised even themselves at their ability to cope. I am inspired by others who have endured more than I have.

Though it may seem counterintuitive, coming to terms with difficult realities can be a source of strength. In his research into parents with children of varying disabilities, Andrew Solomon found that the more serious, incurable, and irreversible the disability, the happier the parents were compared to parents who believed the condition could be treated. He says it is ironic, but "hope may be the cornerstone of misery."

He also found that when parents first accept what they are facing with their child, there is a "psychic reorganization, which is gradual and enduring. It would appear to be true that what doesn't kill you makes you stronger." He also found many parents "who believe that parenting a disabled child has given them knowledge or hope they wouldn't otherwise have had, find worth in their lives." Such parents are able to love, accept, and appreciate their children. Gaining a higher perspective can also help you find meaning and purpose, or at least a deeper understanding of life and humanity. This brings a sense of stability and peace, as well.

In a recent column, David Brooks pondered the meaning of suffering and talked about it in terms of its value. No one would choose suffering going in, but when it comes, people show enormous and admirable ability to face it and even make something positive come from it:

> " . . . seeing life as a moral drama, placing the hard experiences in a moral context and trying to redeem something bad by turning it into something sacred. Parents who've lost a child start foundations. Lincoln sacrificed himself for the Union. Prisoners in the concentration camp with psychologist Viktor Frankl rededicated themselves to living up to the hopes and expectations of their loved ones, even though those loved

ones might themselves already be dead."

He goes on to say that painful experiences change people:

> "Recovering from suffering is not like recovering
> from a disease. Many people don't come out healed;
> they come out different. . . . Instead of recoiling from
> the sorts of loving commitments that almost always
> involve suffering, they throw themselves more deeply
> into them."

My experience as a mother of troubled children has changed me. It has led me to become more spiritual; it has made me calmer and more accepting in a crisis. I am more conscious of living in the now. I am stronger than I ever would have believed I could be. I now believe the urban legend of the mother who raised a car to free her child.

Find a good support group. Whether formal or informal, find a place where others understand. Lean on friends. Look into what services are available through your local community, your church, the school system, and the National Association for Mental Illness (NAMI). Connecting with others in similar circumstances can be a source of help and inspiration. Even more important, it can also be a valuable source of information on ways to get help.

Whether your child suffers from addictions or mental illness, I recommend you try Al-Anon. The focus is to understand and heal from the effects of another's alcoholism; however, its philosophy and help applies to every aspect of life. Meetings are available in most areas every day at every hour. No appointments or signups are required. It is not group therapy. There is no leader, and no one is required to talk. It is simply a peaceful place designed for family members dealing with dysfunction in which, among other things, you will learn from others:

» The difference between helping and enabling

» How important it is to reclaim yourself and your life

» How to detach from your child's behavior with love

» To absolve yourself of self-blame about the dysfunction in your child

» To take care of yourself and stop obsessing about your situation

» That arguing, manipulating, and lecturing are fruitless

I have benefited greatly from all these resources, and know that when things are going badly, the tendency to isolate yourself is hard to resist, but that is when you need a support group the most.

I learned late in this journey that there is a side benefit of taking care of myself, recognizing and meeting my own needs and desires, and changing my attitudes toward my interactions with my emotionally troubled children as well as others in my life. That benefit is that there can be visible and real changes in others. Your emotionally ill child may improve, or at a minimum, there may emerge a healthier dynamic in your relationship.

What about the future?

Often, the greatest worry that plagues and thus undermines us in mind and spirit is this question: What will happen to my child when I'm not around to help care for him? This can be a powerful concern, one that drains a lot of energy out of you. You can help create a sense of inner peace by beginning now to look toward the future, and make even rudimentary plans.

For me, this nagging worry began as I approached my late fifties and my daughter was well into her twenties. It was clear that there would probably not be an end date after which her stable periods would continue permanently. With her continuing need for supervision, especially in the area of managing money for living expenses, counseling, and medical needs, we needed to provide for when that day would come. We didn't want her brothers to have to set aside their own lives to pick up the reins and parent their sister.

We began the process of updating our will, which hadn't been changed since our children were small. We worried about Katherine, who, among other aspects of her life, couldn't manage even small amounts of money. Her math disability made it nearly impossible for her to understand of the simplest daily encounter with money. She had no idea about the costs of things, and the difference between ten dollars and fifty was nearly beyond her comprehension.

As we discussed our situation with the lawyer who was helping us with our will, she strongly advised us about the ARC Trust, something parents of all disabled children might consider and which could alleviate worry about the future. The ARC is a nationwide advocacy program for people with disabilities. One of its programs is a Special Needs Trust. Parents of disabled children establish a financial account for any moneys that come to the disabled person, and the ARC will approve disbursements according to the wishes of the parents and the way the account is set up. In our case, Katherine's eventual share of our estate will go into the trust, and they will manage her money and help her carry on her financial life with those funds. There are trusts operated in most states.

This is a good example of the kind of thing I should have known about, given my many years immersed in the world of disabilities, yet I had never heard of it. Our lawyer told us she had been spreading the word about the ARC for years and found it frustrating how often she would hear that parents didn't know about it.

For more information, go to the website at www.thearc.org.

Share your story. Finally, I can only say that sharing my story and my views has been a helpful adventure for me. There is no comfort in knowing that too many other families are struggling the same way, but helpful insights and practical advice come from being open and talking about our experiences. The simple act of unburdening can be a great relief. Listening to others share ways they have found that make this journey easier is surprisingly helpful. It helps to know you are not alone.

There are a number of websites available for this purpose as well. One in particular may be worth a look. It is called Askforhelp.com and was recently started by Peter Rodger, the father of the University of California Santa Barbara shooter Eliot Rodger. The goal: "About 1 in 4 Americans suffer from mental illness in any given year. It's time we remove the stigma of asking for help. To start, we are providing resources and asking you to share your story so that we may help one another." He goes on to tell his story of being the parent of a son who did "the unthinkable." In the weeks and months since this tragedy, parents, professionals, and the mentally ill from all over the country have shared their experiences and advice on this website.

Sometimes you have to accept the unacceptable. On one of her returns home from months on the street, Katherine was pregnant with her first baby, and the bio-dad was history. Then, out of the blue, a nice young man came into her life and fell for her. He was willing to raise her baby. We had hope that now there would be someone to take care of Katherine and help her to take care of the baby. They eloped. We welcomed him into our family. We helped the couple set up an apartment and bought them a secondhand car so he could use it for work and driving the family around for medical appointments, family visits, and buying supplies and food. For several months, it seemed that maybe a somewhat normal life lay ahead. Katherine seemed happy and stable; pregnancy seemed to wear well on her. Her husband seemed patient and caring. We knew full well that the chances were poor that the marriage would last forever given the circumstances, but at least it seemed to be a good start. The baby would have a name and parents.

We were living in a fantasy world. Mental illness is a pendulum that swings back and forth. I understand better now the term "rapid cycling." In a matter of months, just before the baby was born, there were signs that all wasn't going well for the couple. Katherine began calling me daily to complain about her husband. He wouldn't get a job. They were fighting all the time. He was constantly playing video games or going out with friends. She wanted a divorce. I dismissed her complaints, seeing it all as more of the same kinds of bipolar emotional reactions she had always exhibited. I told her things would get better. She needed to calm down and give her man time to adjust to being married and soon a father. I was completely out of touch with what was happening with my daughter. I could not have anticipated how badly her emotional illness was resurging.

Amazing medical advances in the treatment of HIV-infected mothers made it possible for her to give birth to a healthy daughter. To be doubly sure, the baby would need preventative AZT syrup several times a day for some weeks after birth. Katherine had severe post-partum moodiness. She was irritable and impulsive. She left the hospital too soon while still taking Percocet for pain. When the baby was ten days old, Katherine misunderstood the measuring syringe and overdosed the baby on the AZT syrup. Luckily she was at our house at the time. My husband and I panicked and rushed the baby to the emergency room, while Katherine had a meltdown at home over her mistake. The ER docs had to contact Poison Control to address this unusual and rare medical situation of a six-pound newborn having been given ten times her dose of AZT. There was no treatment other than to wait out the hours until morning with the doctors, watching the infant to be sure of no serious effects. The sight of ER docs trying repeatedly to install a tiny IV needle in a screaming newborn's tiny arm will never leave my memory.

Miraculously, there were no harmful effects, other than on our nerves. The baby was fine.

After that incident, Katherine went into a months-long tailspin, making a series of terrible decisions that will reverberate for years.

Less than a year later, she gave birth to a boy by another man, after a pregnancy marked by homelessness, drugs, and abuse. The bio-dad got deeply into substances, fed Katherine drugs while she was pregnant, then left and married another woman. Just after his son was born, he was arrested and jailed for drug dealing.

Katherine gave birth to two babies in one year by two different men. At this writing, her daughter is in shared custody with us (her parents) and her husband. The new baby, a boy, she is raising alone, because she refused to consider that the best situation for this second child would be adoption. She refuses to get her tubes tied to prevent future pregnancies.

There is no instruction booklet on how to respond to this; no etiquette book for what is the correct thing to do. It is not a celebration. There have been no baby showers. The few people I told about Katherine's first baby offered congratulations, sometimes followed by a question mark. "You will be a grandmother!" people said, and I shrugged, "Well, I guess so." When I told a few people about the second baby, I watched their jaws drop. "Oh, NO!"

It is miraculous that medical advances have made it possible for babies to be born free of HIV. We have fallen in love with Katherine's daughter, and can't imagine her not in our lives. Our connection with her son is more tenuous. We have fear about his future. The time could come when he is not in Katherine's custody, for any number of awful reasons. For the moment, he is safe, healthy, and happy.

I had looked forward to a normal grandparent experience, and this is far from what I had imagined. The inescapable bottom line is, these babies deserve love and should not be rejected because of their origins. Their lives are precious, their futures fragile.

In his book *When your Adult Child Breaks Your Heart,* Dr. Joel Young advises parents that, "Sadly, the ultimate choices for the lives of mentally ill adult children, no matter how impaired they are, always lie with the adult child. This is a very tough lesson for parents to learn, and some people never learn it."

My daughter is making choices and living a life that is far from what I dreamed for her. Her emotional illness makes her unable to hear my advice, my lectures, my frustrations. Now in the mix are two babies whose lives may also take turns that I cannot control.

I have to accept some unacceptable things.

It's Okay to Cry Sometimes

Do all you can. Pray. Think positive. Love your child. Don't give up. But this is a journey on a road with plenty of potholes.

Sometimes it isn't possible to "Keep calm and carry on." "One day at a time" doesn't work, and "Easy does it" is bullshit. And those are the days when you should just go ahead and cry.

Katherine called me one day last year at 7:30 a.m. Her voice wobbled. She was crying. Yet another new boyfriend had just left her injured in her apartment. "He beat me up, and I think my arm is broken." In the chaos of the following hours—the police involvement, the ambulance, the E.R., the X-ray of a fracture of the forearm, the arrest, the pain meds, the "I'm such a screwup!" conversation—I didn't lose my composure. Somehow I stayed strong, calm, and quiet. This, despite the fact that I had already seen bruises on her; despite there having been a mysterious fire in her apartment, despite the holes in the walls from her boyfriend's fits of temper, despite her now having Child Protective Services in her life because of an anonymous caller. I tried not to pile on.

When this terrible day ended, I left her at her apartment and got into my car, and that's when I lost it. I leaned my arms and my head on the steering wheel and sobbed. Would this never end? Would she ever stop making decisions that threatened her survival? How many more of her messes would her father and I have to clean up? How much more of this could I take?

Months later, in court, I watched my daughter made out to be a crazy liar by a clever lawyer. While they couldn't deny her boyfriend had broken her arm, they painted a picture of him as a kindly, caring person who accidentally caused the injury while trying to "help" her when she was in a crazed frenzy. They never met the violent, manipulative boyfriend who had a previous history of violence and had been controlling and abusing her for months. He escaped consequences and moved on with his life. Katherine still fears him and suffers PTSD episodes when she sees a car like his in her neighborhood.

When I think of my baby being harmed this way, it is hard to fight the tears. And maybe I don't have to. Sometimes tears are all I have.

Survive. Even thrive. My world can be a sorry place at times, but when I look at the big picture, I am a lucky woman with much to enjoy in my life. Sometimes I like to see in my mind's eye a balancing scale, with one side the joys and the other side the pain. When I do this, I see that it is easy to focus on the terrible things that happen and the fear for what lies ahead. These dark things loom large. However, I can shake them off, because the scale actually tips in favor of the joys of my life. Is it denial? Perhaps. But I have been able to maintain a clear-eyed assessment that tells me the joys far outweigh the painful times. I try to think about that every time I get discouraged. This is more than survival; it is living a pretty good life. Not a perfect life, but enough.

An old English proverb says, "enough is as good as a feast." Works for me.

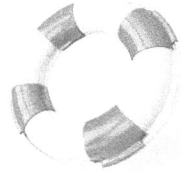

CHAPTER FIFTEEN

If I Ruled the World

*"...the federal government needs to make good
on the unkept promise that President Kennedy and the
Congress made in the 1960s when they pledged
to create a national network of community
mental health centers. . . . Every community needs
a local facility where someone with mental problems
can go for help before he ends up in trouble."*

—PETE EARLEY, *Crazy: A Father's Search
Through America's Mental Health Madness*

Mental Illness Unaddressed

Peter Earley served as a member of the task force that investigated the Virginia Tech shootings. He has cited the progress made in Europe, which considers the individual's potential for danger, referred to as a "need for treatment" standard. This "would enable relatives, police and mental health professionals to intervene earlier. But until our nation builds and funds a community-based mental health system that provides user-friendly treatment oriented toward recovery, the threat of mass shootings will not be reduced."

Earley wrote this before Newtown:

> In a *New York Times* follow-up to the January 25, 2014, random shooting in a Maryland mall by Darion Aguilar, age nineteen, once again we learn of mental illness that was not addressed. "Mr. Aguilar told a general practitioner in April 2013 that he was hearing 'nonviolent and nonspecific' voices. The doctor told . . . Mr. Aguilar to get help . . . but it is not clear if he ever did so."

Again and again, we hear of mental illness unaddressed, with tragic consequences.

The Wishes of the Mother of a Child Who is Mentally Ill

If I ruled the world:

»   *Mentally sick people and their parents would not be on their own* to find help. An unstable person would not be left alone in his crazy world and would find no stigma to asking for help.

»   There would be *a comprehensive clearinghouse of information* that everyone would know about, so that families could easily find the right kind of help, and it would be easy to access. The parents of a troubled child would not have to endure an ongoing crash course in diagnosis, medication, counseling methods, behavioral health and education programs, support groups, and the horror called medical insurance. Parents would not be forced to decimate their home equity, IRAs, or savings in a continuing merry-go-round of failed efforts.

» There would be enough competent, caring people in the behavioral health profession so that *experienced professional help would always be available to meet the need* in every corner of the United States. They would be highly trained and enjoying ongoing professional development so that they would always know of the latest in their field.

» *Treatment professionals would be employed and salaried by a hospital or community health center or medical group.* They would not have to deal with insurance companies. They would not have to charge for missed appointments, a problem that is one of the symptoms of the mentally ill.

» Mental health professionals who encountered a troubled person would coordinate care with others. *Professionals would work in teams* and share expertise with their colleagues and staff. Their clients would never make a call and get voicemail, because someone familiar with them would always be available. No psychotherapist would ever not know or care about a former patient, because information would be available, accessible, and shared.

» *HIPAA and other privacy rules would be modified* so that information would never be kept from family members or doctors who needed it to properly care for a patient. Information must be made more easily available and shared. A psychiatrist who only prescribes medication would be able to keep close monitoring of the non-physician treating counselor for success or failure of a medication regimen, rather than relying on the mentally ill patient or his family. How else can treating professionals know if they are doing the right thing if they don't have real time information?

» *Insurance companies would be out of the mental health business;* financial considerations would never stand in the way of a family getting help. Obtaining mental health treatment quickly is often as urgent as that for a heart attack or a gunshot wound or a stroke. The worst question in the world when trying to find help for a suicidal teenager is "What kind of insurance do you have?"

I don't rule the world, but that doesn't mean some of my wishes for change couldn't come true some day. It does mean massive numbers of those in positions of power need to step up and get involved. This means YOU.

Some Good Things that are Already Happening

All is not lost or hopeless. There are good people out there trying to bring about change. Following is a short list of some recent efforts:

Six-time Academy Award nominee **Glenn Close** discovered that members of her own extended Connecticut family had a various psychological illnesses, some of which ended in suicide, some that had never been recognized or named. As a result, she has used her celebrity status to start a program called **Bring Change 2 Mind**, which seeks to de-stigmatize mental illness, because that is a first step toward openness and seeking treatment.

* * *

Because of his personal experience, **Creigh Deeds** has introduced legislation in Virginia to improve the state's mental health system. This bill requires the upgrading of the qualifications and requirements for mental health workers who evaluate people in crisis, increasing the amount of time a person may be held under an emergency custody order (ECO) from several hours to between twenty-four and seventy-two hours as in other states. Also, Deeds calls for the establishment of a digital registry to have real-time information about available psychiatric beds, and he calls for a comprehensive study of the mental health care delivery system, which he has said "killed" his son.

* * *

Television journalist **Jane Pauley,** who has openly discussed her own experience with bipolar disorder, has sponsored the **Jane Pauley Community Health Centers** in her hometown of Indianapolis. They offer comprehensive, affordable medical services, including behavioral health screenings and treatments.

* * *

The parents of one of the children who died at Sandy Hook Elementary School have founded the **Avielle Foundation,** funded through donations and grants to promote the idea that "mass killings can be prevented by studying brain health." In addition, two other parents of those children, Mark Barden and Nicole Hockley, have established **Sandy Hook Promise,** which is a multifaceted nonprofit organization with the goal of enlisting communities to prevent future such horrors.

* * *

A theater production called **This is My Brave** is being performed around the country on a regular basis (http://thisismybrave.org). Created by Jennifer Marshall, who also writes a blog titled BiPolarMomLife about her struggles with mental illness, it is a program in which people to talk openly about their experiences of mental illness. "We believe that each time one of us shares our story, there's another crack helping to break down the stigma of mental illness. Right now, it's time to *be brave* and bring mental health issues into the spotlight because they've been in the dark too long." Kevin Earley, the subject of his father Pete Earley's book, is a member of the board of this unique organization and performs as part of the show, which can be viewed on YouTube.

* * *

Former Rhode Island Representative **Patrick Kennedy** championed in Congress the Wellstone-Domenici Mental Health Parity and Addiction Equity Act of 2008 to required mental illness to be covered by health insurance plans at the same level as physical illness. Since leaving Congress, he has devoted his efforts to **"ONE MIND™** , an independent, non-partisan, non-profit organization that is working on research into mental illness and brain disease. He knows firsthand from his own and his family's experience about mental illness, addiction, and brain disease, and he recently published a memoir about his experience titled *A Common Struggle*. He believes brain research should be as important and supported as President Kennedy's stated goal of going to the moon in the early 1960s.

* * *

Mental illness is brain illness. Sometimes, brain dysfunction is related to an injury, or possible damage from other causes. Psychiatrist **Dr. Daniel Amen** has been doing research with single photon emission computed tomography (SPECT) brain scans since 1991 and has found that "mild traumatic brain injuries are a major cause of psychiatric illness that has ruined peoples lives" (TED talk, 2013). He believes that medicating patients based on symptoms without looking at their brains is the wrong approach. He believes that recent shootings can be attributed to mental illness treated with medication and no analysis of what was happening in the brain. In a recent talk, he was asked about the diagnosis of NFL players of brain damage from continuous trauma and concussions, which made the news connected with the late Frank Gifford and updated medical theories about O.J. Simpson. Dr. Amen's advice is radical: Don't let your kids play football, soccer, wrestling, or anything else that will involve frequently bumping their heads. Personally, if I were raising my children anew, I would listen to him. There are several **Amen Clinics** in the United States that perform SPECT brain scans and offer appropriate treatment.

The need is understood and the goal is in place. Across this country there are worthwhile efforts happening, but they continue the tinkering around the edges that has brought us to this place. What is needed is a broader, more comprehensive overhaul of the mental health system.

We Know What Needs to be Done

As Pete Earley said in the wake of the Creigh Deeds tragedy, "We don't need another task force. We know what needs to be done." As these things go, a task force was named anyway.

No more studies. Nor more reports. No more looking the other way because "it can't happen to me." Or "it can't happen in my neighborhood." It IS happening in your neighborhood. No more defending the system as it is, saying we can't afford to do more. We are already spending too much to incarcerate the mentally ill. In my state of Virginia alone it is estimated that 6,000 mentally ill people are in prison, getting no treatment.

The next question is always: How do we fund the change that is needed? When there is a national will, we find a way. A war in Iraq, a financial stimulus for the Great Recession, a rescue for banks and car companies. When something MUST be done, it gets done.

If I were in charge, things would change. Big time.

1. We need a national system of networked community centers for care of the mentally ill. Every community needs such a center, which would:

» Be a fully funded, state-of-the-art treatment center, like a hospital ER.

» Be open, 24-7, 365, where people in need of attention would be treated immediately by a mental health professional.

» Have a bed available for any and all patients in crisis.

» Be able to access records of the patient's physical and mental health history immediately, including contact information for previous treatment professionals.

» Have a fully stocked pharmacy on-site so that meds are immediately available.

Long-Term Care: If, after local crisis intervention, it is determined that a patient needs long-term residential care:

» The community center would be linked to high-quality, affordable residential programs within each state. Note the word "linked."

» Staff members at both ends of this transfer would be thoroughly familiar and have a relationship among professionals and programs, so they know which centers are a good fit for which patients and can make recommendations and referrals.

» Treatment professionals who staff the inpatient programs would communicate directly and thoroughly with those who have referred, treated previously, or will be treating after discharge.

» A step-down follow-up treatment plan would be linked, to include group living arrangements for disabled but functional people.

» Such group homes would be available for those who needed them.

2. Collegiality Among Mental Health Professionals: Independent mental health professionals—social workers, psychiatrists, psychologists, psychotherapists—must change. It is a calling, a mission, and a way to make a living, and I pray each practitioner is successful, but it cannot work if it becomes just a profit-making venture.

» Professionals must become collegial and work in teams.

» As part of their licensing, they should be required to participate in a network that regularly meets to share information and update each other about what is happening in the mental health field.

» They must continually update their knowledge of what is available for treatment in their area and beyond, so they can make informed recommendations to patients and their families.

» They should do some of their work in the community centers.

» They must confer and discuss their patients, within the constraints of privacy laws, so that each case is not reinventing the wheel.

3. Forced Hospitalization/Treatment: Legislators must become aware and make changes to the laws that make it so difficult to force a mentally ill family member into treatment. If my child can be on my medical insurance until she is twenty-six, or even forever if it is determined that she is disabled, then I, as her parent, should have more say in her treatment. If I could have forced my daughter to stay in the hospital in Texas, she might not have HIV today. If I could have forced her to stay in the hospital in Massachusetts, she might not have become pregnant with a second child when she was unable to care for the first. My hands were tied by the unintended consequences of rules developed to protect the mentally ill, which in such instances actually prevent them from getting into treatment.

4. Who Pays? Insurance and Money: No person in need of treatment should find paying for it to be an obstacle. Insurance companies should work directly with treatment professionals, community centers, and hospitals, with no copays or deductibles for the patients. For a mentally sick person on the street, even a five-dollar copay is an insurmountable obstacle. Since community centers would be addressing community problems, the community should pay for much of it, ideally in a private-public partnership. Treatment would be offered on a sliding scale. Practicing counselors would be free to have private practice and charge what they want, but they should be required to work part-time in the community health centers pro-bono or at a salaried rate.

Connectivity: Uncle Walt's Idea

In the twenty-first century, when every individual can be immediately connected to anyone on the planet anywhere anytime, there would be connectivity among physicians, psychiatrists, counselors, social workers, pharmacists, school officials, mentors, insurance companies, hospitals, clinics, and group homes. The chances of a single mentally ill person becoming a functional member of society would greatly increase if such connectivity existed. It would allow sharing and documentation of ideas and information about treatments, medications, concurrent family issues, school events, or traumas suffered. It would prevent starting from scratch with each new practitioner and program, relying on memory or personal recordkeeping to bring the new "helper" up to speed. Discouragement borders on despair as parent and child ride the bumper cars of new faces, places, and therapies while the illness gets worse.

The Disney Corporation offers an example of using technology for the kind of connectivity needed in the mental health field. They have recently instituted a new system of "magic wrist bands" for visitors to wear that contain all the information Disney needs to ensure they have a great vacation: room key, charge card, ID, park admission, and more, so they can keep data on preferences and activities. Information is accessed by a mere tap of the band against a receiver pad. Setting aside privacy issues for a moment and simply focusing on the technology, if this can be done for entertainment, it is obvious that it could be useful in other areas, such as medical information. Disney is teching up, and other institutions should be doing the same. "The company must aggressively weave new technology into its parks . . . or risk becoming irrelevant to future generations."(*New York Times*)

One of the most successful recent developments in similar technologies is wearable fitness bracelets, which in 2014 were estimated to be on 2.7 million wrists. The most successful of these items, designed for monitoring of healthy activities, is the Fitbit. This little item tracks how many steps one takes in a day, or how many calories one consumes, among other capabilities. It syncs such daily information with a laptop or smartphone. It is everywhere, and becoming more common every day. The Apple Watch is another new development, which amounts to a nano-computer on one's wrist.

So much potential here. Setting aside cost considerations (not a small concern, since the Fitbit alone is $100 and the Apple watch could be in the thousands), it would seem a no-brainer that one's medical information could and should available in the same way. The good news is the nonstop speed of these kinds of new developments in technology are gradually making their way into the medical field. However, even at the high speed of change that is happening, it isn't yet enough to address the need, especially when it comes to mental illness. Change needs to happen—yesterday.

We Need a Movement

A network of interconnected mental health centers should not and cannot be solely a goal; it needs to become a movement. Every family, every neighborhood, has been touched by mental illness. This movement needs a leader, someone who will be out there every day making this a priority of the national consciousness. Such a leader must be committed to ensuring the fulfillment of the promise made by President Kennedy fifty years ago for community mental health centers and decent group housing to replace the asylums of the past. Every corner of the media should be working every day to get the information out to the public so that not a day goes by without Americans hearing about this effort and feeling a part of it.

People out there are working on this issue, but this country needs so much more.

If I ruled the world, could mental illness be prevented or cured? Probably not. Would random shootings by unbalanced young men be eliminated? Probably not. But it is not too much to ask for humane, comprehensive, competent, and caring treatment for those who need it. Schizophrenics would not be sleeping on steel grates on city sidewalks. Families of those who need help would not be on their own to search for solutions to manage an unmanageable problem, made worse by lack of information. Many people with emotional disability could hold jobs, live in decent housing, helping each other in group homes, making untold positive contributions to our national life. Parents would not have to decimate their home equity and retirement savings in failed treatments and hospitalizations of their children. Treatment professionals could see more successful outcomes in their life's work. Communities could feel safer.

With committed effort, funding, technology, and leadership, the mental health of this country could be managed well. But first, each of us has to own it.

CHAPTER SIXTEEN

Coping Strategies: Laughter, Faith, and Hope

"Fear is the lock; and laughter the key to your heart."
—STEPHEN STILLS

"If we couldn't laugh we would all go insane."
—JIMMY BUFFET

Laughter: Part of the Treatment Team

A man was walking in the street one day when he was suddenly attacked, brutally beaten, and robbed. As he lay unconscious and bleeding, a psychologist who happened to be passing by rushed up to him and exclaimed, "MY GOD! Whoever did this really needs help!"

* * *

I'm not being crude or disrespectful when I make jokes about my kids or the situation or even the tragedies. The laughter that is common in our household is a blessing. We all have a good sense of humor. Mel Brooks once said that, "Humor is just another defense against the universe." When the universe sends you lemons, you make lemonade, sweetened with humor. Scientific studies show the actual physical healing power of laughter, so when things get tough, watch a Marx Brothers movie, hang out with your funniest friends, go to a comedy improv show.

There have been many tough moments when the quick wit of one of our family members has leavened the moment and made it less unbearable. Of course, the humor is dark. But whatever works. Friends have heard me say more than once, "I gotta laugh, else I'd be crying."

Our default family joke when faced with something that doesn't make sense is a pause followed by a simple comment: "JPN." It sums up the moment as "just plain nuts." It is taken from an old Gary Larson cartoon:

So what is funny about mental illness? An organization begun in Canada in 2004 called Stand Up for Mental Health (SMH) finds the humor in it. The program teaches people with mental illness how to do standup comedy to use humor as a form of therapy. The SMU program is designed to lessen the stigma and help people with mental illness feel better about themselves. A documentary about SMH titled *Cracking Up* won a government VOICE Award in 2008.

A study of more than 500 comedians recruited from comedy clubs, agencies, associations, and societies largely in the United Kingdom, United States, and Australia demonstrated that people who are good at making others laugh share some personality traits with bipolar disorder and even schizophrenia. While not all comedians suffer from mental illness, a number of them have been open about it, suffering depression, "the idea of the sad clown." One woman who participated in the survey said, "If you do have issues, then comedy is often the way of getting you through." This was particularly true of the comic genius Robin Williams, who suffered from addiction and depression for years and eventually committed suicide, yet was one of the most talented and accomplished actor/comedians in the entertainment world.

Make light of a bad situation? Why not?

Example: Coping: or, I'm Drinking and I Don't Care Who Knows It. My therapist once asked me how do I cope with everything going on in my family? I answered, "Shopping, travel, good food, good books, writing, seeing friends. Oh, and wine—is that bad?" He answered, "That's what it's for."

It reminds me of one of my first lessons in handling parenthood. Pre-children, we were at a Saturday afternoon summer picnic with two other couples and their toddlers. One runny-nosed two-year-old began whining and tantruming over something. His mom looked thoughtful for a moment, then grabbed the wine bottle from the cooler and began to pour. "There's nothing wrong with that child that another glass of wine for ME won't cure."

So my wine intake has increased somewhat over the last decade. Too much?

My aching brain says, "Compared to what I face every day, does it matter?" And I pour another glass.

Have Faith (Religion Not Necessary)

Surviving this journey is helped if the burden can be lifted, even a little. When you don't feel isolated and alone, hope can blossom, even slightly. Having a feeling of spirituality, of a universe larger than one's daily earthly sorrows, is important. While it helps sometimes to have a church or a God in your life, even agnostics can benefit from being open to this minimal, yet enveloping and comforting, philosophy.

Worry about sons who have problems is stressful, but worry about daughters is stressful to the nth power, because they can get pregnant. From the age of eighteen on, my daughter was increasingly promiscuous and as careless about birth control as she was about taking her psychiatric medications. I told her many times that if she got pregnant she could not count on us to help in any way. I finally persuaded her to get the Depo-Provera shot that would last several months at a time and didn't require her daily compliance. I kept the calendar and I made sure she went to the doctor for her shots, and this worked well for a while.

Then she disappeared for several months and her birth control lapsed. When she returned home, she was pregnant.

"She has to have an abortion." Anyone completely aware of the situation (except for Katherine) believed there was no other course of action. She couldn't be a mother! Her emotional instability, her learning issues, her inability to hold a job, her untreated HIV infection, her history with moving from relationship to relationship and living on the street, the fact that the bio-father had beaten her within an inch of her life before she left him. Further, how could a healthy baby result from this pregnancy? The reasons were inescapable. As I mentioned earlier, even the BPD specialist we were seeing in Richmond told her, "You cannot have this baby."

She wouldn't hear of it.

It's been widely known that in the Kennedy family, one of the eight children of Rose and Joseph Kennedy, had developmental and emotional problems from birth. When she was a young woman, her parents subjected her to brain surgery—a lobotomy—to control her behaviors. She spent the rest of her life in an institution. I had strong ethical problems with the idea of forcing an abortion on my daughter, just as I had ethical problems with the decision the Kennedy family had made about their daughter. Katherine was over eighteen and insisted on becoming a mother, though everyone familiar with her knew that this could not work. Could. Not. Work.

Further complicating our situation, I am a Catholic, and the position of my church is well known. Katherine has always said she was against abortion, too. Yet I considered forcing her to have the procedure, based on the coming catastrophe. It would take lawyers and a court fight, and I realized that by the time it was settled, she would be well into her pregnancy. Even as a pro-choice mother, I have great reservations about terminating a pregnancy after the third month. I could not have been party to that.

The question of abortion faded quickly when I took her for her first checkup and sonogram. She did not know how pregnant she was; the sonogram indicated she was past thirteen weeks. We both cried as we looked at the image move and the tiny heart beating on the screen. Katherine's tears were joyful. Mine were tears of grief.

Plan B had to be adoption, even though I have come to believe that adoption is not always the happiest outcome of problem pregnancies. In the various support groups I have attended over the years, I have seen too many adoptive parents whose children have serious problems, such as learning disabilities and various types of emotional illness. But given the circumstances in my daughter's case, there was no doubt that adoption had to be the next goal, despite her resistance to the idea. We met with an adoption attorney to have all the information we needed "just in case," but my daughter was determined to keep her baby. She got angry whenever the subject was broached. I feared if we pushed too hard on this issue, she would run away again.

Around this time, I went to Mass one Sunday at a new church, where a pro-life group was handing out brochures about what to do about an unwanted pregnancy.

Their poster said, "WE ARE HERE TO HELP."

After Mass, I approached one of the women, and as I began my story I burst into sobs.

"My daughter is twenty-one and pregnant and needs a safe place to stay, and she needs to be persuaded to adopt."

We sat down in the empty church and she took my hand. She was very sympathetic and told me about a home for unwed mothers not far away. I began to feel a shred of hope. But when I mentioned my daughter's HIV status, she pulled away. "Oh, well, they won't take her then."

My church, the bastion of militant pro-life activism, would not help us.

Though my religion often disappoints me, my faith has not wavered. It has evolved and simplified; the idea that there is a power larger than myself has become stronger. I have come to accept that I am not in charge of the universe, and who or what is in charge can never be understood by the mind of human beings, though we still have the need to try. When I remind myself to think in these terms, it allows me to let go of the burden for a time. Letting go of the idea that I have any power to control my adult children's choices leads to moments when I actually experience a sense of peace about my life and my family. It allows me to see the little joys of each day with gratitude. It isn't easy, and I can't always accomplish this, but it is the right path for any parent with a child who is truly what Andrew Solomon refers to as "unknowable."

I wish I had known this sooner. I am grateful that I know it now. It helps.

LORD OF ALL HOPEFULNESS

Lord of all hopefulness, Lord of all joy
Whose trust, ever childlike, no cares can destroy.
Be there at our waking and give us, we pray
Your bliss in our hearts, Lord, at the break of the day.
Lord of all eagerness, Lord of all faith
Whose strong hands were skilled at the plane and the lathe.
Be there at our labors and give us, we pray
Your strength in our hearts, Lord, at the noon of the day.
Lord of all kindliness, Lord of all grace.
Your hands swift to welcome, your arms to embrace.
Be there at our homing and give us, we pray
Your love in our hearts, Lord, at the eve of the day.
Lord of all gentleness, Lord of all calm,
Whose voice is contentment, whose presence is balm.
Be there at our sleeping and give us, we pray
Your peace in our hearts, Lord, at the end of the day.

JAN STRUTHER, 1901–1953
OXFORD UNIVERSITY PRESS

Hope is a Good Four-Letter Word

"Hope is the only bee that makes honey without flowers."
—ROBERT GREENE INGERSOLL

The optimist in me keeps me going. I try to think positive, and I still have hope.

Becoming a parent is the ultimate expression of hope. Cynics believe that hope is just disappointment deferred. But I'm an optimist, and optimists find hope in every new day. For me, hope has been the life ring I've held white-knuckled through years of very rough seas. Hope is the reason a parent does everything possible to help a child with special needs, whether physical health problems, learning disabilities, autism, addiction, mental illness, or anything else.

You gotta have hope. When it comes to my children, hope and love are interchangeable. Dreams may die, but I can replace them with new ones. When you are the parent of a child with mental illness, that fact is a constant. Every time you think the worst is behind you, some new crisis rises like a tsunami. This is the nature of the beast. But once that wave has passed, you clean up the mess and move on to new goals, new hopes. The purpose of this book is to tell those people who are just beginning a difficult journey that it is survivable. And if the message of this book affects the world of mental health, maybe they will not only survive, but even do well. It begins and ends with hope.

* * *

"If you want to feel rich, just count all the things
you have that money can't buy"
—UNKNOWN

It's easy to say and nearly impossible to do sometimes, but it can salvage a terrible moment. My hope and optimism help me focus not on what is missing in my life, but on what I do have. This is what I mean when I say that experiencing hell helps you see heaven.

At this writing, Katherine is stable. For several years, she has been under the care of the Amen Clinic of Reston, Virginia, where she was initially extensively tested. They scanned her brain twice in their large SPECT machine. An inch-thick report showed her to have signs of trauma and failure in the frontal lobe, where impulsivity and reactivity are supposed to be controlled. She's described as having "no brakes." She has been treated with some new ideas, such as hormonal and nutritional approaches. As often happens with psych meds, against medical advice, she went off the prescribed Lamictal some time ago, yet it seems there is little difference. The recent progress she has made leads her to believe she has a future in which she can manage both her mental and physical illnesses.

My marriage has survived forty years when statistics were not in our favor. Too many relationships fail in the face of intractable family problems. Some research indicates a much higher divorce rate for parents of special needs children. My husband and I still cling to each other's strength despite all we've been through with our kids, as well as other grenades that have been thrown at us by life, such as cancer and job loss and financial struggles and emergency room visits, as well as aging parents and deaths of friends and other loved ones.

AIDS is not a death sentence. Good medications are keeping Katherine alive and healthy so she can work toward the best life she can create for herself. In a world where babies in other countries are often born with AIDS and a death sentence, she has given birth to two healthy children, free of HIV, a miracle that wasn't possible even a decade ago. Katherine has not given up on her life, despite many reasons to do so. She still has dreams and goals, despite regular setbacks. At this writing she has just graduated from a year-long hair stylist school, and she hopes to make it a career. She is taking care of herself and takes her HIV meds consistently.

Katherine is doing a good job as a mother. Despite everything, she learned painful lessons about her limitations in the aftermath of giving birth to her daughter. With much support and help from us as well as community services, she has been raising her son mostly alone. He is healthy and happy. She is often lonely, because friendships and romantic relationships are difficult for her to maintain. However, she is working through all of this with counseling, hoping ultimately to form a "normal" family life for herself and her son. She has not been able to re-establish a permanent connection with her daughter, but she is working on that as well.

My two sons who did not have the emotional disability are thriving and happy. Both personally and professionally, they have attained amazing and unique accomplishments at young ages, beyond what I ever could have imagined for them. One is married and the father of a new baby girl, working in California in the movie business. The other worked at the White House before he was twenty-five. Having troubled siblings and war-weary parents has not held my boys back, and they demonstrate their support, love, and pride for our entire family in everything they do. They make us proud each and every day.

Joy in a grandchild. Katherine's daughter, our granddaughter, lives with us under our legal guardianship. With the consent of her parents, we are in the process of legally adopting her, as ours is the only home she has ever known. The child that came out of such dire circumstances is unaware that her life is unusual. She happily spends time with her father and his parents, as well as on visits with Katherine and her half-brother. She is a delightful child: smart, beautiful, and fun. She brings me laughter and gives my days a purpose unlike any other time of my life except when I was raising my own babies. I can't imagine her not in my life. What else in the world offers as much hope as a baby? What else offers perfect joy as her smile?

* * *

A Word about Brendan

When I started writing this book in 2013, it was intended to be a memoir that would offer some coping strategies and a message of hope. I wanted to share my experience and convey to other parents my firm belief that it is possible to survive, even thrive, while raising a child with learning disabilities, mental or emotional illness, or addictions. Two of my four children hit the DNA jackpot and endured combinations of all of these challenges. For my husband and me, it has been a long and difficult journey to nurture, educate, and protect two adored children who for years were following increasingly dangerous collision courses with catastrophe. I was ready to write this book because my son had overcome serious problems to become successful in an amazing way, and my daughter, though still many steps behind, was making slow but steady progress. The first draft of my book was almost ready for prime time.

Then, on September 8, 2014, a terrible phone call came. Our son Brendan, who had just celebrated his thirtieth birthday, who had rebuilt his life and accomplished soaring academic success, who was in a serious relationship with a brilliant and beautiful medical student who might have become his wife, had died in a tragic freak accident while studying overseas in Rome. The young man who had conquered paralyzing anxiety and self-medication that turned to dangerous addiction, whose adventurous exploits had already cheated death many times, was gone.

The shock paralyzed me for days, and the sorrow and horror preoccupied my mind for many weeks. It helped a little to receive many heartwarming messages from his friends all around the United States and abroad. They blessed us with stories of how he touched their lives; how much he was admired and loved for his brilliance, his courage, kindness, humility and humor. As part of his own recovery, he had counseled many others; there were people who came to his funeral who told us that he literally saved their lives. We have learned that we were not the only people who understood what an extraordinary individual he was.

Daily living has slowly and gradually returned to a new kind of normal. There is no path forward other than acceptance and to go on living.

When this first happened, my thought was that I could never complete my book. The random unfairness of my son's death seemed to undermine my purpose. However, after much thought on this, I came to the conclusion that I couldn't allow this terrible event to eclipse my message of hope to other parents. I remembered that more than a year ago, when I told him I was writing this book about his sister, he said, "Write about me, too." And so I included him in my story. Following is what I wrote of him before the tragedy:

Brendan has always done things in a big way. At birth he was over eleven pounds and was born so quickly he nearly made his appearance in the car. He appeared with "the caul" over his head, which the doctor said was a sign of good luck. We liked that.

Throughout his childhood he was always larger than his peers. He adored his older brother and followed him everywhere, but he didn't talk much, and so earned the nickname "mystery man." Eventually, as he emerged with a personality quite different from our first boy, we came to calling him "our different-drummer kid," which became a more-than-appropriate moniker as he grew up.

In third grade, his teacher told us she thought he was gifted, especially in math, which was a surprise, because he kept that hidden. He began to demonstrate some social anxiety in kindergarten. Later, he became a class clown in school and began to drive his teachers crazy. Only his fourth grade teacher seemed to see his potential and appreciate his uniqueness, but most found it maddening for a bright student to take nothing seriously, not do homework, and answer essay questions with sarcasm:

» Fifth grade religion class: "Question: Describe the effect Jesus Christ had on the world. Answer: No effect."

» Ninth grade cooking class: "Question: Describe the recipe for soda bread. Answer: Soda. Bread. One human toe."

At age fourteen, he was already over six feet tall, failing in school, withdrawn, and unable to demonstrate a bit of introspection about his problems or feelings. He did drawings that showed a dark but brilliant Edmund Gorey-type world view. He was still a mystery, and we were surprised when a battery of neuropsych tests yielded a genius IQ. (Once again, as with his sister, we did not recognize the true nature of what was going on inside our child's head, despite thinking we knew it all.) The tester told us that someday he could become the only expert in the world in one obscure thing, indicating some Asperger's tendencies that could ultimately make him famous. This young man had extraordinary potential.

"Potential" became meaningless when he spent his teen years getting into trouble. We tried to change his path; there was counseling, boarding school, an array of programs, There was addiction and relapse. He became so reckless and immune to help that the unthinkable became a thought: Instead of a future of graduations, weddings, and birthdays, we might have to plan his funeral. Yes, we went there. One counselor told us "this could have a bad end."

With the help of counselors, we finally had to let go and leave it to him to change his path. And, miraculously, in his early twenties, he changed course. For the first time, he entered rehab on his own volition, walking in and telling them, "Help me. I can't live like this anymore."

Afterwards, he served two years in Americorps, working to improve the lives of at-risk teens and young people in a small rural town out West. As he regained his confidence, he set aside his doubts about whether he could catch up and finish college. He had already started and dropped out of three different schools, but he went back and quickly completed his undergraduate degree with honors, while taking up running and participating in marathons for charity, and working as a counselor to those suffering from addiction. He followed his under-grad work immediately with grad school, attaining a master's degree in eighteen months while traveling the world and soaking up the experiences of a lifetime in just a few years. He is now a doctoral candidate in history, accepted at Kings College in London. Even with all he has accomplished, he remains humble. When he received his acceptance to Kings, he was amazed. "Imagine!" he said, "Me, of all people. Barely finished high school. And I'm on my way to the Harvard of the UK!"

He is an affable, witty, knowledgeable, brilliant, and eccentric polymath. In his spare time, he is a musician, hilarious storyteller, and a world champion online Scrabble player.

He is also a young man still rushing to catch up and regain lost time. He has been living large: snowboarding in the Alps, running with the bulls in Pamplona, visiting a distant cousin piano maker in Prague, hanging out in Kiev during the Ukraine crisis, standing on the Great Wall of China, flying in a hot air balloon over the Atlas mountains in Morocco, racing on a camel across the desert. He visited Beijing, Moscow, and Kuala Lumpur on a student study trip that also took him to North Korea. He is one of only a small number of Americans who have visited the captured ship *USS Pueblo* and seen the DMZ from the north side. His return itinerary included a stop in Cambodia, and a flight took him from Katmandu over Mount Everest. You can't get larger than that.

* * *

Like all parents who have lost a child, there is no getting over this. There will be no cure for the grieving, but a scar will make it less of an open wound. His siblings grieve quietly, for fear of causing their parents pain. We don't talk about him much, to keep the grief at bay, but also because though he was easy to love, he was not easy to know or understand. His older brother said recently, "Brendan was too brilliant for this world." There will be a very large empty chair in our family forever, but the joy of our pride in his miraculous accomplishments despite his personal issues can never be diminished.

His legacy will go on into the future. In connection with his love of travel, his appreciation for knowledge and study, and for experiencing all that the world has to offer, we established a scholarship in his name at the Claiborne Pell Center for International Studies at Salve Regina University in Newport, Rhode Island.

My message of this book remains: If our son could survive to accomplish his personal goals of getting physically and emotionally healthy, reconnecting with family, finding a good woman to love, making a difference in the lives of others, achieving academic honors, seeing the world, and bringing back honor to his name, then all things are possible.

Resources

ABC's 20/20. Barbara Walters interview with John Hinckley, Sr. 4/28/1983.

Allison Bottke. *Setting boundaries with your adult children.* 2008. Harvest House Publishers.

American Psychiatric Association—www.psychiatry.org

Andrew Solomon. "The reckoning." *The New Yorker,* March 2014.

Andrew Solomon. *Far from the tree.* 2012 Scribner

Bill Booth, theinteractgroup.com/blog, 2016

BrainyQuote.com

Bringchange2mind.org

David Brooks. "What suffering does." *New York Times,* April 7, 2014.

Debbiebayerblog.com

Dr. Daniel Amen. TED Talk. October 2013. YouTube

Dr. Joel Young. *When your adult child breaks your heart.* 2013. Lyons Press, Guilford Connecticut

"Dr. Phil Talks to Ted Williams about Entering Rehab." www.youtube.com, January 13, 2011.

E. Fuller Torrey, M.D. and Judy Miller. *The invisible plague: the rise of mental illness from 1750 to the present.* Rutgers U. Press, Piscataway, NJ, 2001.

Foxdc.com

George McGovern. *Terry: My daughter's life and death struggle with alcoholism.* New York: Penguin Group, 1996

Jacquelyn Martin, AP Photographer, USA Today 1/5/14

John Green. *The fault in our stars.* 2012. Dutton division of Penguin.

Justin Torres. "In the reign of King Moonracer." *Washington Post Magazine,* November 15, 2013.

Letters to the Editor, Dr. Michael Lustick, *New York Times,* 1/20/2015.

Lynne Shallcross. *Counseling Today, publication of the American Counseling Association.* www.counseling.org. "Taking Care of Yourself as a Counselor," 1/17/11.

Matthew Lysiak. *Newtown: An American tragedy.* 2013: Gallery books.

Mental Illness (Opposing Viewpoints). Greenhaven Press, Farmington, MI, 2012.

National Alliance on Mental Illness (NAMI) website—www.nami.org.

National Association of Community Health Centers—www.nachc.com

National Institute of Mental Health website—www.nimh.nih.gov

New York Times, 3/12/13 "Columbine Said to Influence Gunman at Maryland Mall"

New York Times, 1/25/2016 "Where Addiction Treatment Programs Are Taking Shape"

One Mind website—http://www.1mind4research.org

Parent Child Resource Center, Derby, Connecticut—www.lnvpcrc.org

Paul R. Linde, MD. *Danger to self: On the front line with an ER psychiatrist.* 2010. University of California Press.

Pete Earley. *Crazy: A father's search through America's mental health madness.* 2006 Putnam Adult Publishers.

Petula Dvorak "Let's connect the dots on mental illness before the violence occurs." *Washington Post,* 9/19/2013; and "Devastating toll of mental illness demands our attention," *Washington Post,* 1/20/2014.

Psychcentral.com. "Things not to say to someone with mental illness." 4/29/2013.

Psychologytoday.com July 2011, Marsha Linehan.

Robert Whitaker. *Anatomy of an epidemic: Magic bullets, psychiatric drugs, and the astonishing rise of mental illness in America.* Crown Publishers New York, 2010

Sandy Hook Promise. www.sandyhookpromise.org

Standupformentalhealth.com.

Susan Klebold. *A Mother's Reckoning: Living in the Aftermath of Tragedy.* 2016 Crown.

Susannah Cahalan. *Brain on fire: My month of madness.* 2013, Simon and Schuster.

T.M. Luhrmann "Redefining Mental Illness." *New York Times,* 1/17/2015.

thereseborchardblog.com

thisismybrave.org

Treatment Advocacy Center, Arlington VA. "Involuntary Treatment is Warranted for the Severely Mentally Ill."—www.treatmentadvocacycenter.org.

U.S. Department of Health and Human Services website.

http://aspe.hhs.gov/health/reports/2013/mental/rb_mental.cfm

USlifeexpectancy.com

Virginia Pilot—Hampton Roads.com. "Virginia family's lawsuit puts scrutiny on ADHD diagnoses." May 12, 2014.

William Styron. *Darkness visible: a memoir of madness*

MARY C. McKAY is a writer, teacher, mother of
four, and grandmother of three. She has written
for militarybratlife.com and allvoices.com.
She writes about popular culture, parenting,
mental illness, education, and politics, and she
is working on a middle-grade novel.
Her blog is truthaccordingtomary.blogspot.com.
Mary has a Bachelor's degree in psychology
from the University of Rhode Island and a
master's degree in education from the University
of Virginia. She lives in McLean, Virginia,
with her husband and granddaughter.